Essential
Costa
Blanca

by Sally Roy

Sally Roy is a freelance Scottish travel writer
with a long-held affection for the south of
Spain, where she has family ties.
She has written and contributed to numerous
guides on Britain and Europe including *AA
Spiral Spain*, *AA Spiral Venice*, *AA CityPack
Madrid* and *AA CityPack Barcelona*.

Above: *huddled buildings and churches soar above
Alcoy's gorge*

AA Publishing

*Mending modern fishing
nets the traditional way*

Written by Sally Roy
Original photography by Michelle Chaplow
Updated by Mona King

First published 1999
Reprinted 2001. Information verified and updated.
Reprinted May and Sep 2001; May 2002
This edition 2003

Published by AA Publishing, a trading name of Automobile
Association Developments Limited, whose registered
office is Millstream, Maidenhead Road, Windsor, Berkshire
SL4 5GD. Registered number 1878835.

A CIP catalogue record for this book is available from the
British Library.

ISBN 0 7495 3574 1

The contents of this publication are believed correct at
the time of printing. Nevertheless, AA Publishing accepts
no responsibility for any errors, omissions or changes in
the details given, nor for the consequences of readers'
reliance on this information. This does not affect your
statutory rights. Assessments of the attractions and hotels
and restaurants are based upon the author's own
experience and contain subjective opinions that may not
reflect the publisher's opinion or a reader's experience.

We have tried to ensure accuracy, but things do
change, so please let us know if you have any comments
or corrections.

A01088

Find out more about
AA Publishing and the
wide range of services
the AA provides by
visiting our web site at
www.theAA.com

Colour separation: Pace Colour, Southampton
Printed and bound in Italy by Printer Trento S.r.l.

Contents

About this Book

Essential *Costa Blanca* is divided into five sections to cover the most important aspects of your visit to Costa Blanca.

Viewing Costa Blanca pages 5–14
An introduction to Costa Blanca by the author.
　　Costa Blanca's Features
　　Essence of Costa Blanca
　　The Shaping of Costa Blanca
　　Peace and Quiet
　　Costa Blanca's Famous

Top Ten pages 15–26
The author's choice of the Top Ten places to see in Costa Blanca, listed in alphabetical order, each with practical information.

What to See pages 27–90
The three main areas of Costa Blanca, each with its own brief introduction and an alphabetical listing of the main attractions.
　　Practical information
　　Snippets of 'Did you know…' information
　　3 suggested walks
　　4 suggested tours
　　3 features

Where To... pages 91–116
Detailed listings of the best places to eat, stay, shop, take the children and be entertained.

Practical Matters pages 117–24
A highly visual section containing essential travel information.

Maps
All map references are to the individual maps found in the What to See section of this guide.
For example, the Sierra de Espuña has the reference ✚ 28B2 – indicating the page on which the map is located and the grid square in which the Sierra de Espuña is to be found. A list of the maps that have been used in this travel guide can be found in the index.

Prices
Where appropriate, an indication of the cost of an establishment is given by € signs:
€€€ denotes higher prices, €€ denotes average prices, while € denotes lower charges.

Star Ratings
Most of the places described in this book have been given a separate rating:

✪✪✪　　　Do not miss
✪✪　　　　Highly recommended
✪　　　　　Worth seeing

Viewing
Costa Blanca

Above: *the pale sand and azure sea of Calpe*
Right: *a fisherman's wife selling shellfish, used in local rice dishes*

Sally Roy's Costa Blanca

Mountainous Benimantell – as much the face of the Costa Blanca as the busy coastal resorts

The Language

Much of the Costa Blanca lies in Valencia, an autonomous province which recognises two official languages, Valencian and Spanish, whose dominance varies from place to place. You may hear either spoken, and will certainly notice both if you are driving; so be prepared for different spellings of the same place and warning signs in either language. Place-names in this book are given in Castilian Spanish first, followed by the local Valencian spelling in brackets.

Most visitors to the Costa Blanca head for Benidorm, knowing that the Mediterranean's biggest resort will provide an unforgettable holiday. Many tourists find everything they need in the coastal resorts – an agreeable year-round climate, a good standard of accommodation and plenty to do.

But the Costa Blanca has much more. A few kilometres from the tourist centres traditional Spain re-emerges, a country where historic towns are set amid superb scenery and the rural pace of life remains undisturbed. Finding this other side is a challenge and delight, and the memory of this will last long after the tan has faded.

It is a land of huge variety, with thriving ports, bustling cities and a vast agricultural industry. Life has changed immensely in the last 50 years, but its people remain fiercely proud of their region, their history, their traditions and their culture. For most visitors though, the main attraction will be the beauty and fertility of the land. High sierras soar above terraced valleys planted with almonds, oranges and olives. Discover the vineyards, hidden upland streams, and vistas of buff, red and ochre peaks. Explore the still lonely coastal stretches, where pines shade rocky paths and the air is scented with aromatic plants. Gaze over the salt flats, haunt of wading birds, a flat and shimmering landscape backed by miles of rich market gardens. The sooner you discover this Costa Blanca, the more you'll enjoy this lovely corner of Europe.

Costa Blanca's Features

Geography and Climate

• The Costa Blanca officially lies along the coastline of the region of Valencia, but this book includes the hinterland and the region of Murcia.

• At 325km, the Segura is Spain's eighth longest river.

• Espuña, with a height of 1,579m is the area's highest mountain.

• There is one regional park and several natural parks, including marine reserves, within the area.

• The northern part of the Costa Blanca enjoys 3,147 hours of sunshine annually, and the southern 3,098 hours.

• The annual rainfall ranges from 394 to 148mm and occurs mainly in the winter months.

People

• The population of the area is over 2,350,000, most living in the cities and their suburbs.

• Only around 50 per cent of the area's inhabitants were born here of local parents.

• Over 70 per cent of foreign property owners are English or German.

Agriculture and Industry

• The main fruit crops are oranges, lemons, cherries, peaches, nectarines and loquats.

• Large amounts of almonds and olives are grown here and are important Spanish exports.

• Local produce includes rice, tomatoes, peppers, courgettes, beans, aubergines and a range of salads, which are exported throughout Europe.

• Fruit and nut processing are major industries.

• Shoe manufacture is an important source of revenue.

Fresh fruit and vegetables in a street market

Defining the Boundaries

Since Spanish decentralisation and the establishment of the autonomous regions in the 1980s, the Costa Blanca strictly speaking is now only the area within the region of Valencia. The Murcian coast, running from San Pedro del Pinatar to Aguilas, is officially divided into the Costa Cálida in the north and the Costa del Almería in the south.

Below: *chatting in the sun*

Essence of Costa Blanca

Holiday life on the Costa Blanca revolves around sun, sand and sea, with plenty of good food and a few late nights. If this is your first visit here, soak up the sun and the atmosphere, sparing perhaps a couple of days for exploring the beautiful inland mountains and one or two atmospheric towns. Once you have tasted the diversity of the region, you will probably return and gradually get to know the hidden corners, where traditional Spanish life has remained untouched by the glitz of the big resorts.

Below: *grapevines still thrive on traditional Moorish terraces*

Bottom: *clean beaches lie within an easy stroll of Costa Blanca's modern hotels*

The 10 Essentials

If you are visiting the Costa Blanca for the first time or have only a few days here, make time for at least some of these essentials:

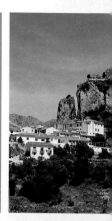

• **Bake in the sun** on a sandy beach or enjoy a swim off one of the rocky headlands on the northern coast.

• **For lunch, fill up** on a selection of *tapas*, delicious bar snacks ranging from fresh seafood, *tortilla* and olives, to dried ham, grilled fresh garden vegetables and salted almonds.

• **Explore inland** from the coast and discover hilltop villages, lush market gardens, historic towns and splendid mountain landscapes.

• **Pass an evening Spanish-style:** take a stroll along a palm-lined boulevard, have a leisurely drink, do a little late shopping, have dinner at 10:30 and listen to some live music.

• **Take the scenic Costa Blanca Express** between Alicante (Alacant) and Dénia for great views and glimpses of small-town life; or hop on at night and have dinner up the coast from your resort.

• **Take a boat ride** for fresh breezes and a change of scene, to the offshore island of Tabarca, Benidorm Island, or the islands in the Mar Menor.

• **Go to a local market** and admire the produce, smell the flowers and buy a picnic, a paella pan or a pair of locally made sandals.

• **Have a gastronomic day out** sampling local wine, locally grown rice, almonds and honey, and *turrón*, a super-sweet nougat produced here to be eaten at Christmas.

• **Take in a fiesta**, be it the pre-Lenten *Carnaval*, the Holy Week processions, a Moros y Cristianos parade commemorating the Reconquest, or a summer firework display.

• **Eat a traditional rice dish** – fish-based on the coast, or with pork, game and vegetables inland.

Top: *the crags of Guadalest rise above the roofs of this picturesque village*

Above: *an Alicante flower stall glows with warm southern colours*

The Shaping of Costa Blanca

Moor and Christian statues in Caravaca recall the early struggle to expel the Muslim invaders

orange, peach and almond orchards planted; date palms, rice, sugar cane and cotton cultivated. Cartagena, Murcia and Játiva (Xátiva) expand – still known by their Moorish names.

1095
Start of Berber invasions; Moorish Spain becomes a province of the North African Berber empire.

1212
First decisive Christian victory against Moors in northern Spain; start of the Reconquest.

1243
Murcia is conquered by Ferdinand III and becomes part of Castile.

1238–48
Jaime I of Aragon gradually ousts the Moors from Alicante.

1492
Expulsion of the last Moors from Granada by Ferdinand and Isabella, the Catholic Monarchs. Expulsion of Spanish Jews.

1500–c1650
Repeated Berber pirate attacks along the whole eastern coast of Spain.

***c*50,000 BC**
First evidence of cave dwellers in painted caves at Villena and Benidoleig.

***c*1000**
Phoenicians establish trading centres; Játiva (Xàtiva) and Elche (Elx) date from this period. The Phoenicians introduce the pottery wheel.

***c*650**
Greeks establish trading colonies along the coast and introduce olives, grapes and figs.

500
Carthaginians invade Spain; Cartagena, which they call *Quart Hades*, is founded and becomes their main power centre. Gold and silver are mined in the vicinity.

218–201
Second Punic War; Hannibal marches his Carthaginian troops along the Costa Blanca, through France and over the Alps. Rome invades; the Latin language, from which Spanish developed, is introduced.

AD 555
Roman empire collapsing; Visigoths emerge as dominant power for the next 100 years.

711
Moors invade the Spanish peninsula through Gibraltar and occupy Alicante (Alacant) by 718.

718–1095
Moorish occupation: irrigation and paper manufacture introduced;

1519
Revolt against nobility and persecution of *Moriscos* (converted Moors) in the kingdom of Valencia.

1609
Expulsion of *Moriscos*.

1701–14
War of Spanish Succession between Philip of Anjou and Charles, Duke of Habsburg. Philip's claim to Spanish throne is ratified by the Treaty of Utrecht.

1808–12
War of Independence (Peninsular War) against the French.

1812
First Spanish constitution is written.

1833–36
Present provincial boundaries are fixed, establishing Alicante and Murcia in their modern form.

1858–62
Rail line from Madrid to Murcia and Alicante built.

1923
Miguel Primo de Rivera becomes dictator.

1931
Alfonso XIII goes into exile.

1936–39
Spanish Civil War; Alicante and Murcia remain Republican.

1939
General Franco, the leader of the Nationalists, becomes *caudillo* (leader) of Spain.

1960–70
Tourism booms on the Costa Blanca; in Alicante visitor numbers rise from under 100,000 a year to over 3,750,000.

1975
Juan Carlos becomes King of Spain.

1982
Valencia (which includes Alicante) and Murcia established by statute as autonomous regions.

1986
Spain becomes part of the European Community with the fastest-growing economy in western Europe.

Early 1990s
Recession throughout Spain.

1999
The Partido Popular party wins again in Valencia and Murcia in regional government elections.

2002
Introduction of the European single currency; the peseta is replaced by the euro.

The castle of Almansa – one of many ancient strongholds

Peace & Quiet

The dappled Queen of Spain fritillary butterfly

As in so many parts of Spain, tourism in the Costa Blanca clings to the highly developed coastal strip, leaving the hinterland virtually untouched. Less than 8km inland from even the busiest resort, Spanish rural life continues as it has always done. So if you crave tranquillity you never have far to go, with the added bonus that this lovely coast is backed by some wonderful countryside.

Above: *dramatic and unspoilt cliff scenery near Benidorm*

Below: *the high sierras abound with reptiles like this big-eyed lizard with its young*

The Coast

Even beside the sea there are still undeveloped pockets where you can have a swim, rock scramble or a clifftop walk far from the sights and sounds of the 21st century. There are some impressive pine-studded cliffs and solitary coves south of Cabo de la Nao (Cap de la Nau, ➤ 61), stretches of dune-backed secluded sand between Alicante (Alacant) and Torrevieja, and remote, empty bays and beaches at Calblanque (➤ 16) below Cabo de Palos, now a designated natural park. These coastal areas have an exceptionally rich spring flora; lavender, thyme, rosemary, white, yellow and pink cistus, and other aromatic plants carpet the cliffs from March to June. Some parts of the coastal water have remarkable submarine life, which flourishes on the expanses of sea grass, and includes the now-rare turtle. The salt flats around Santa Pola and Torrevieja provide rich feeding for more than 250 species of birds, including good-sized flamingo colonies.

The Hinterland

South of Alicante the area behind the coastline is relatively flat and very fertile, planted with vegetable crops and huge orange groves, the landscape dotted with small farms and sentinel palm trees. The palms form a forest around Elche (Elx, ➤ 38), thousands of trees carpeted with cool greenery, where you can stroll in shady peace. South again, Murcia seems like one vast market garden, the upper Segura valley (➤ 90) a rolling landscape of peach orchards, olive groves and rice fields interspersed with patches of woodland, steep escarpments and sleepy country towns, its quiet roads bordered with the vibrant colours of poppies, crown daisies and Bermuda buttercups. This agricultural landscape provides shelter for a good range of birds and small mammals – naturalists keen on insects and small reptiles will find fascinating life in the stone walls and long grasses bordering the well-tended fields.

The Mountains

North of Benidorm the high sierras rise precipitously from the coast, wonderful mountain systems of great drama, the bare rockfaces glowing with different colours as the light changes throughout the day. The lower slopes of these great mountain valleys have been intricately terraced since Moorish times and are planted, as they have been for centuries, with almonds, oranges, loquats, cherries and olives. Roads twist up through the mountains, sometimes clinging to the hillsides, sometimes allowing stupendous panoramas of valleys and further chains of peaks and rockfaces. These hills are laced with ancient footpaths offering magnificent day-long hikes for discovering the wildlife, birds and flora. Foxes, rabbits and other mammals are hard to spot in daylight, but the soaring birds of prey, migrant wintering songbirds and prolific insect life add an extra dimension to walking in this superb landscape.

Right in the south of the region lies another great mountain area, the Sierra de Espuña (➤ 26), a superb mountain chain covered with natural pine woods.

Above and below: the quiet hill roads of the Sierra de Espuña are ideal for cyclists and walkers

Walking
Mountain walking in the sierras is becoming increasingly popular, and there are good publications and tourist office leaflets available. Remember to let someone know where you are going and when you expect to be back, wear suitable clothes and footwear, be prepared for the weather to change, and take plenty of water and something to eat. Detailed maps are available from Servicio del Instituto Geográfico Nacional, General Ibáñez de Ibero, 28003 Madrid. Local tourist boards will also have suggestions and leaflets and can put you in touch with the relevant local groups.

Costa Blanca's Famous

Artists

This part of Spain has given birth to many eminent Spaniards, who have made their mark on local history. World famous are the writer Gabriel Miró Ferrer, who was born in Alicante (Alacant), and Murcia's most famous son, the 18th-century sculptor Francisco Salzillo. Salzillo specialised in life-size painted wooden figures, which adorn altarpieces and are used in religious processions throughout Murcia.

Nobles

One particularly notable local family of the north, the Borjas of Játiva (Xàtiva), Italianised their name to Borgia when they settled in Rome. A powerful aristocratic family, a branch later moved to Gandía where they built themselves a sumptuous palace. The Roman Borgias flourished, producing two popes, Calixto III and his nephew, Alexander VI, both supreme practitioners of nepotism. Alexander was instrumental in carving up the New World between Spain and Portugal and also fathered a son, the notorious Cesare. This stylish but infamous man, on whom Machiavelli modelled *The Prince*, conspired to have his brother murdered and was involved in constant sexual intrigue and power politics.

Salzillo's Jesus of Nazareth, *Museo Salzillo*

Working Visitors
During the late 1950s and early 60s a number of films were made in the Alicante area; the stars included Peter Ustinov, Terence Stamp, Trevor Howard, Elsa Martinelli and Hayley Mills. A couple of decades later professional golfers, including Nick Faldo, Bernhard Langer, Seve Ballesteros, Ian Woosnam and Tiger Woods are frequently seen playing in European tournaments on the Costa Blanca golf courses.

The Rich and Famous

Today, tourism has changed the Costa Blanca forever, and the 19th- and early 20th-century travellers who explored this coastline would scarcely recognise it. One of the last people to write about the area before the boom was Rose Macaulay, who travelled along the coast and described sleepy villages which are now buzzing resorts and a landscape which has virtually ceased to exist. The luxurious villas, hidden in pine woods above the sea, are the retreats for northern European celebrities, business people, financiers, sportsmen and women and their families. Many famous people have found the area ideal for a second home, where they can escape the attention of the media which is an inevitable part of life in their own countries.

Top Ten

Above: *vibrantly coloured oranges – one of the Moors' great legacies*
Right: *a bronze relief in a corner of Alicante's Castillo de Santa Bárbara*

1
Calblanque

✚ 29D1

✉ 70km east of Murcia

🍴 Bar occasionally open in summer (€)

🚌 Bus from Cartagena or La Unión to La Manga and 30- to 50-min walk

ℹ Small information office in park. Irregular opening hours
☎ 968 36 25 13

♿ None

↔ Cartagena (➤ 85), Mar Menor, La Manga and Cabo de Palos (➤ 86–7)

A remote and untouched stretch of coast, Calblanque has secluded bays and beaches, flowers, birds and solitude.

A few kilometres south of the highly developed resorts around the Mar Menor lies one of Spain's most unspoiled coastal stretches, Calblanque. Local people fought hard in the 1980s to protect this area, which is now a designated natural park.

Access is down a bumpy track off the busy main road running to La Manga. Within minutes, the roar of traffic disappears, hills rise up and the road gradually winds down to the sea. From the small car park boardwalks lead across the fragile dunes to the beaches, and paths run along the coast in either direction. If you are looking for an unspoilt beach, this is it. The fine sands and crystal-clear water are only part of the experience, and it's worth leaving the beach to walk along the coast or explore the inland hills. A track runs south towards Cabo Negrete and the lighthouse at Punta Negra. Follow it down to see impressive rock formations caused by water erosion, lovely views and tempting swimming coves. The waters here are wonderfully clear and limpid, with protected underwater vegetation and sea creatures – perfect for keen scuba divers and snorkelers. A scramble in the hills behind the coast will give you an idea of the incredible richness of Calblanque's flora and fauna. Apart from other walkers, you may meet a herdsman and his goats, which graze on the aromatic plants.

Calblanque's main attraction is its peace, and its survival as an unspoilt enclave is a good example of what determined public opinion can achieve.

Calblanque's lovely coastline and uncrowded beach lie well off the beaten track

2
Castillo de Santa Bárbara, Alicante

This should be the first stop on a tour of Alicante and is a perfect way to get your bearings, while admiring amazing views of the town and coastline.

The impressive fortifications of the Castillo de Santa Bárbara

The rambling complex of fortifications known as the Castillo de Santa Bárbara dominates Alicante (Alacant) from its position on the summit of Monte Benecantil. Rising dramatically on a bare rock above the town, the castle is best viewed from the oldest quarter of Alicante, the *villa vieja*, in the Barrio de Santa Cruz.

The site has certainly been fortified since prehistoric Iberian times and the Carthaginians, Romans and Moors all built here from the 3rd century BC. No traces of their work remain and today's structures date mainly from the 16th century. The castle was repeatedly attacked but proved impregnable until the War of the Spanish Succession; assaulted from the sea in 1706 by Sir John Leake, it fell to Philip V's French troops in 1708, and was blown up by them in 1709, killing the English garrison. Undeterred, the English returned a century later and occupied the castle throughout the Peninsular War.

Today, the main attraction is the superb view from the top, a vast panorama over the town, from the palm-shaded Explanada through the 19th-century streets and shady plazas to the old quarter, and up and down the coast with its curving white beaches, headlands, port and marina. You can walk, drive up or take a lift from the Playa del Postiguet which ascends through a shaft cut into the hill.

33B5

Above Playa del Postiguet, Alicante

965 16 21 28

Apr–Sep 9–7 daily, Oct–Mar, 9–2, 4–7. Closed Sun pm and Mon. Lift operates at same times

None on site

G, S

Alicante: Rambla Méndez Núñez 23
965 20 00 00

Good

Castle free; lift moderate

Catedral de San Nicolás de Bari (➤ 32), Ayuntamiento (➤ 32), Museo de Arte del Siglo (➤ 32), Barrio de Santa Cruz (➤ 35)

17

3
Gallinera Valley

✝ 29E5

✉ 50km north of Benidorm

🍴 Choice of restaurants
and bars (€–€€€)

🚌 None

ℹ️ From any of the
northern resorts

♿ None

❓ Moros y Cristianos
festival, Planes, 1st Sun
in Oct. Most
villages have
their annual
fiesta during
Aug

↔ Alcoy (► 36),
Cocentaina
(► 62)

*One of the loveliest of valleys, Gallinera is best
seen when the blossom of the almond and cherry
trees cloaks the slopes in pink and white.*

The dramatic mountains behind the northern Costa
Blanca are cut by valleys, some narrow and steep, others
broad and gentle. They are all exceptionally fertile, meticu-
lously terraced where needed and irrigated by a system
devised by the Moors. These valleys are nicknamed after
the main crop: the Gallinera has long been known as the
Cherry Valley.

A twisting and scenic road runs inland from Pego the
whole way up to the village of Planes, passing through

Top: *luscious cherries are
sold at the roadside in the
Gallinera valley*

Above: *most country
houses have a fig tree
planted near by*

superb landscapes. The land was first settled and culti-vated by the Moors and you can still trace their influence in the names and layout of the villages. The *Moriscos*, Christianised Moors, stayed on here after the Reconquest and were only finally expelled in 1609. The terracing on the hillside is often Moorish, and walkers can find the ruins of their dry-stone houses. The valley is heavily planted with cherry trees, iridescent green and white in spring, speckled with crimson fruit in summer, and interspersed with orange, almond and olive trees. Towering above are the dramatic escarpments and peaks of the sierras, with seductive little roads twisting up the hillsides.

The main settlement is Planes, a white, quintessentially Spanish village, perched on a hill below a ruined 12th-century castle, with a 16th-century aqueduct and a hidden blue swimming hole in the valley below.

The other tiny villages like Alcalá, Margarida, Benialfaquí and Benitaya all have their charms, their traditional way of life a perfect antidote to the more strident, upbeat attractions of the coastal resorts.

Bottom and inset: *slopes rise steeply above rural villages like Planes*

4
Guadalest

An excursion inland from Benidorm to this Moorish castle, encircled by mountains, makes an ideal early evening outing.

From this angle the fortress of Guadalest still seems impregnable today

🕂 29E4

✉ 28km northwest of Benidorm

☎ 965 88 50 95

🕐 10:30–6

🍴 Bars and restaurants (€–€€€)

🚌 From Benidorm

ℹ Benidorm: Avenida Martinez Alejos 16
☎ 965 86 81 89

♿ Few

✋ Moderate

↔ Fuentes del Algar (➤ 65), Guadalest Valley (➤ 66), Polop (➤ 72), Sierra de Aitana (➤ 74)

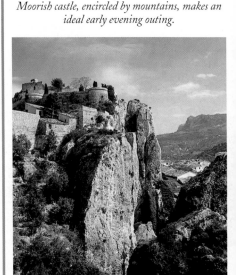

The mountains of the Sierra de Aitana rise steeply behind Benidorm's coastline, towering above lush and fertile valleys and dotted with hilltop villages. These valleys were terraced and irrigated by the Moors, who built a network of castles from which they controlled the northern valleys.

The most dramatically sited of these fortress villages is Guadalest, perched on a rocky crag above terraced orchards and a lake. Driving inland from the coast, the best view of its castle and bell tower, seemingly precariously balanced on the summit of a spectacular rock, is from the almond terraces and olive groves on either side of the twisting road. A few further bends and you reach the 15th-century Moorish castle, surrounded by a maze of narrow streets, whose only access is by a tunnel cut through the rock. Steep slopes drop to the reservoir below, and across the water the mountains, speckled with vegetation and cut by thread-like tracks, soar up over 1,066m.

Athough this castle was never overrun, Jaime I of Aragon took it after a lengthy siege in the 13th century. It successfully repelled Charles, Duke of Habsburg, during the War of the Spanish Succession and survived an earthquake in 1644. Attractions include small museums and gift shops.

5
Huerto del Cura, Elche (Elx)

This fascinating botanical garden within the great palm forest of Elche is perfect for shady relaxation after a few hours' sightseeing.

Stately palms and luxuriant shrubs surround the Dama del Elx

Thousands of date palms surround three sides of the historic inland city of Elche, one of only two palm forests in Europe. Probably originally planted by the Phoenicians in the 4th century BC, these magnificent trees are still watered by the 10th-century irrigation system built by the Moor Abderraman III. The palms have infiltrated the city, providing shade and bursts of cool green wherever you look. Within this vast forest some areas have been transformed into gardens and parks, the most famous of which are the Huerto del Cura, or Priest's Grove, and the beautifully manicured municipal park.

Laid out in the 19th century, Huerto del Cura palms shelter stands of orange and pomegranate trees, and paths wind past glorious displays of cacti and lilies. Beside a lily pond deep in the garden stands a replica of the bust known as the Dama del Elx, a mysterious and enigmatic Iberian figure dating from 500 BC and discovered in 1897 at the nearby hamlet of La Alcudia. The original is now in the Museo Arqueológico in Madrid.

The most famous tree is the Imperial Palm, a vast and ancient hermaphrodite with seven stems, six male and one date-bearing female, growing from one main trunk. The date crop from specific trees has traditionally been for consumption by famous Spaniards; two palms regularly supply King Juan Carlos and Queen Sofía with dates.

29D3

Porta de la Morera, Elche, 25km southwest of Alicante

Summer daily 9–8:30; winter daily 9–6

Bar (€)

E

Elche: Plaça del Parc
☎ 965 45 27 47

Very good

Moderate

Elche (► 38)

6
Montgó & Cabo de San Antonio

Dénia's pretty waterfront is backed by the soaring mountains of Montgó

An unspoiled oasis of natural beauty, Montgó offers a chance to appreciate how this coastline and hinterland appeared before the tourist boom.

✚ 29F5

✉ 40km north of Benidorm

☎ Information centre 966 42 32 05, Spanish-speaking only

🍴 Choice of restaurants and bars in Jávea and Dénia (€–€€€)

ℹ Jávea: Plaza Almirante Bastarreche 11, Aduanas de Mar ☎ 965 79 07 36, and Plaza de la Iglesia 6 ☎ 965 79 43 56. Dénia: Oculista Buigues 9 ☎ 966 42 23 67

♿ None

↔ Dénia (► 63), Jávea (► 71)

Easily reached from the holiday centres to the north and south, the massif of Montgó and the promontory of Planes run down to the Cabo de San Antonio to the north of Jávea (Xàbia). This whole area, covering more than 2,000ha, was designated a natural park in 1987, mainly because of its flora. Within the park more than 600 species of wild flowers grow, many of them unique indigenous sub-species. It is a sheer delight to wander the flower-bordered tracks and paths, breathing air scented with wild rosemary and lavender and murmurous with bees. White, yellow, purple and pink predominate, the low-growing shrubs punctuated by miniature palms, heather, juniper, ilex and pines. The park has much bird life, with some rare gulls along the coast and birds of prey on higher ground.

For serious hikers, there is demanding walking up to the 753m summit, with sweeping views up and down the coast, while the less energetic can enjoy several low-level routes. These mainly run through Planes, once heavily cultivated with raisin-vines and still scattered with small-holdings. A cypress-lined track takes you to Los Molinos, a line of old windmills above Jávea bay, last used in 1911. The walk (or drive) out to the lighthouse at the cape gives an opportunity for more lovely views and a chance to see the ruins of the tiny 14th-century hermitage dedicated to Saint Anthony, after whom the cape was named.

7
Peñón de Ifach

Peñón de Ifach is a dramatic headland soaring over 300m up from the azure sea and dominating the sandy beaches on either side.

No photograph can capture the impact of the huge craggy outcrop, flanked by bustling family beaches, that rears up from the sea at Calpe (Calp). This is the Peñón de Ifach, the symbol of the Costa Blanca, a looming mass of limestone, geologically related to Gibraltar's rock and linked to the mainland by a sandy isthmus. Legend claims Hercules first charted the Peñón, and the remains of Roman Calpea lie on its slopes. Ifach was certainly used as a watchtower, with warning fires lit on the summit, during the years when the Berber pirates threatened the coast, and it was later renowned as a smugglers' haven. Today, despite the teeming summer crowds on Calpe's lovely beaches, it remains isolated and untouched, thanks largely to its modern role as a natural park.

A climb to the 330m summit is best tackled in the cool of the morning in the summer; the views along the coastline and inland to the sierras are at their best around sunrise. Allow about 45 minutes to reach the top, along the track which runs through a tunnel in the bottom of the rock face. The gentler lower slopes run down to rocky inlets and tiny bays, and are brilliantly carpeted in spring with a profusion of over 300 species of wild flowers and plants, including an orchid unique to the Peñón. Bird life is prolific here; in winter the rare Audouin's gull is a frequent visitor and flamingos inhabit the nearby salt flats, along with a variety of waders.

29F4

Calpe, 20km northeast of Benidorm

Bars and restaurants in Calpe (€–€€€)

Ifach Charter ☎ 965 10 25 91 summer only

Calpe: Avenida de los Ejércitos Españoles ☎ 965 83 69 20 and Plaza del Mosquit s/n ☎ 965 83 85 32

Calpe (► 62)

The rugged mass of the Peñón soars above the sands of a Calpe beach

8
San Feliu,
Játiva (Xátiva)

 29D5

✉ Carretera Castillo,
Játiva, 60km north of
Alicante

🕐 Apr–Sep, Mon–Sat
10–1, 4–7, Sun 10–1;
Oct–Mar, Mon–Sat
10–1, 3–6, Sun 10-1

🍴 Choice of restaurants
and bars near by (€–€€€)

🚌 Tourist train from
outside the tourist
office Mon–Sat 12:30,
4:30, Sun 12, 1, 4:30

🚆 From Alicante via Alcoy

ℹ Alameda de Jaume I, 50
☎ 962 27 33 46

♿ None

✋ Free

↔ Collegiata Basílica de la
Seu, El Castell, Museo
Municipal del Almudí
(► 68)

*The rich colours of San
Feliu's main altarpiece
contrast with the church's
simple interior*

*An ancient and beautiful church, San Feliu is in a
lovely position on wooded slopes overlooking the
historic town of Játiva.*

One of the region's finest religious buildings, lovely and
evocative San Feliu (Sant Feliu) is set among olives and
cypresses below the walls of Játiva's historic castle. A
must for fans of early architecture, this ancient church
stands on the site of a 7th-century palaeo-Christian church,
the seat of the Visigothic bishopric.

The present building, one of the oldest in Valencia, was
erected in the 1250s on the orders of Jaime I, soon after
his expulsion of the Moors. It has a single nave, split by
four massive arches, and architecturally is surprisingly
similar to Syrian churches of the same date. Only rarely
used now for services, the church's walls are hung with
superb Spanish Renaissance religious paintings, mainly
from nearby churches and monasteries. Some are sadly in
need of restoration, but the colours and gilding still glow.
The altarpiece was commissioned at the end of the 15th
century and shows scenes from the life of Christ and the
Virgin, flanked by images of Saints Cosmas and Damian,
two early saints, and Saint Blaise, the patron saint of sore
throats. The holy water stoup is carved with scenes from
the Nativity, including a shepherd leading two rather
charming pig-like sheep. Along the external entrance walls
runs a loggia, its roof supported by six Roman columns.

9
Santa María, Murcia

The façade of this lovely Mediterranean Gothic cathedral is the finest among Murcia's many examples of baroque architecture.

Murcia's cathedral, dating from the 14th to 18th centuries, stands out in a city crammed with exuberant baroque architecture. If ever a building captured the spirit of the place, Santa María, with its ebullient and lavish decoration and sense of religious fervour, surely does.

The cathedral's south side retains its Gothic façade, but the main west front was rebuilt after a flood in 1735. Designed by Jaime Bort, this feast of curves and swooping detail, only slightly restrained by its soaring Corinthian columns, is liberally dotted with statues of gesticulating saints, their robes tossed by some celestial wind.

The interior, retaining signs of its Gothic origin, is an extravagant example of florid plateresque. The high point is the Capilla de los Vélez, completed in 1507 and designed as a funeral chapel for a powerful local family. With its lovely screen and rich vaulting this must be one of Spain's finest examples of Hispano-Gothic architecture. Other highlights include an urn containing the heart of 13th-century Alfonso the Wise in the Capilla Mayor and a 600kg gold and silver processional monstrance in the cathedral's museum. The choir contains a *Christ* by Murcia's famous 18th-century resident, Francisco Salzillo. He specialised in realistic polychrome wooden figures to be used in Holy Week processions; his work can be seen at the Museo Salzillo (▶ 80). A ramp and stairway leads up the 98m 18th-century tower, which has great views.

✚ 79B1

✉ Plaza Hernández Amores 2
☎ 968 21 63 44

🕐 10–1, 5–7

🍴 Choice of bars and restaurants near by (€–€€€)

🚌 26, 28, 39, 49

ℹ Plaza del Romea 4
☎ 902 10 10 70

♿ Good

✋ Cathedral free; museum moderate

↔ Casino (▶ 79), Museo de Bellas Artes, Museo Salzillo, San Juan de Dios (▶ 80)

Exuberant baroque detail on the exterior and interior of the cathedral of Santa María

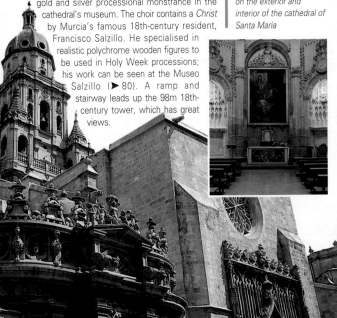

10
Sierra de Espuña

✝ 28B2

✉ 25km south of Murcia

🕐 Always open

🍴 Summer-only bar in park, restaurants and bars at Alhama and Aledo (€–€€€)

🚌 From Murcia to Alhama

ℹ Information in summer from the Casa Forestal de Huerta Espuña inside the park. Murcia: Plaza del Romea 4
☎ 902 10 10 70

✋ Free

↔ Aledo (➤ 84), Totana (➤ 90)

A springtime view of the high tops of the Sierra de Espuña

The contrast between the rocky peaks and pine forests of this high sierra and the coast below makes a day in this park an enjoyable change.

Southwest of Murcia city, the Andalucian sierras tail off into a series of rocky massifs, undeveloped and undiscovered. This is the Sierra de Espuña, one of Spain's renowned natural parks, a wilderness area of dramatic peaks and pine forests offering scenic drives, serious climbing and superb walking.

The forest was the inspiration of Ricardo Codorniú, an engineer charged in 1891 with finding a solution to the frequent and destructive floods which swept down from the sierra to the villages below. Huge areas of hillside were planted with Canary pine, cypresses and cedars, which stabilised the slopes and created this unique habitat. Over the last century more than 250 plant species have established themselves, and the forest is the home of wild boar, deer, mountain cats and tortoises, as well as more common woodland creatures. At 1,579m, the ochre peak of Espuña dominates the whole park area, frequently glimpsed through the trees from the road which runs through the park from Alhama to Aledo. This narrow, steep and tortuous road is one of Murcia's most beautiful, and gives access to different areas of Espuña. Waymarked walking trails run through the woods, tracks give access to challenging rock-climbs, there are shady glades with natural springs and well laid-out picnic areas.

What to See

Above: *ripening almonds in an orchard*
Right: *preparing for a busy day at sea*

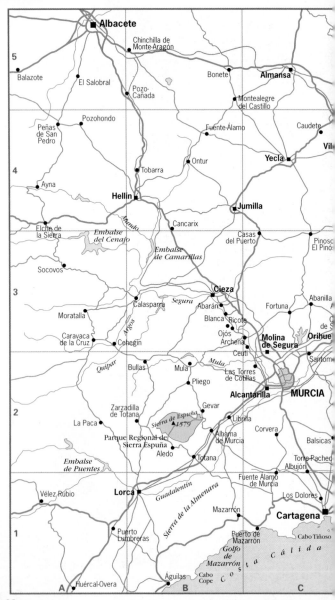

5

Balazote

El Salobral

Pozo-Cañada

■ Albacete

Chinchilla de Monte-Aragón

Bonete

Almansa ■

Montealegre del Castillo

Caudete

Peñas de San Pedro

Pozohondo

Fuente-Álamo

Vil

4

Ayna

Tobarra

Hellín ■

Ontur

Yecla ■

Jumilla ■

Elche de la Sierra

Embalse del Cenajo

Socovos

Cancarix

Embalse de Camarillas

Casas del Puerto

Pinosc El Pinó

3

Moratalla

Caravaca de la Cruz

Calasparra

Cehegín

Segura

Cieza ■

Abarán

Blanca Ricote

Ojós

Archena

Ceutí

Fortuna

Abanilla

de S

Molina de Segura

Orihue

Argos

Quípar

Bullas

Mula

Mula

Santom

Pliego

Las Torres de Cotillas

Alcantarilla ■

MURCIA

2

La Paca

Zarzadilla de Totana

Sierra de Espuña ▲1579

Gevar

Librilla

Corvera

Balsicas

Parque Regional de Sierra Espuña

Aledo

Alhama de Murcia

Totana

Embalse de Puentes

Fuente Álamo de Murcia

Torre-Pached Albujón

Vélez Rubio

Lorca ■

Guadalentín

Mazarrón

Los Dolores

Cartagena ■

1

Puerto Lumbreras

Sierra de la Almenara

Puerto de Mazarrón

Golfo de Mazarrón

Cabo Tiñoso

Costa Cálida

Huércal-Overa

Águilas

Cabo Cope

A

B

C

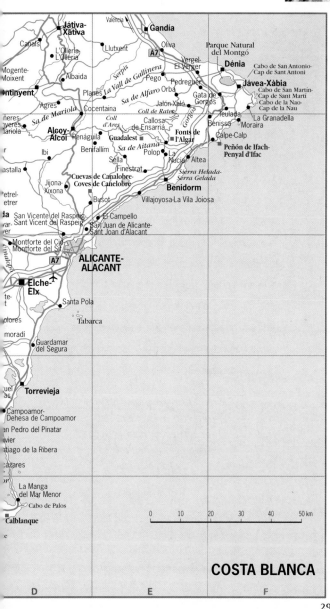

Canals
Játiva-Xàtiva
L'Ollería
L'Olleria
Valencia
Gandía
Oliva
Llutxent
Parque Natural
del Montgó
Vergel-
El Verger
Pego
Dénia
Cabo de San Antonio-
Cap de Sant Antoni
Jávea-Xàbia
Cabo de San Martín-
Cap de Sant Martí
Cabo de la Nao-
Cap de la Nau
La Granadella
Mogente-
Moixent
Albaida
Serpis
La Vall de Gallinera
Planes
Sa de Alfaro Orbá
Pedreguer
Gata de
Gorgos
Jalón Xaló
Coll de Rates
Moraira
Ontinyent
Agres
Cocentaina
Teulada
Benisso
Sa de Mariola
Coll
d'Ares
Callosa
de Ensarriá
Fonts de
l'Algar
Calpe-Calp
ineres-
ineres
ariola
Alcoy-
Alcoi
Peñáguila
Guadalest
Penyal d'Ifac
Peñón de Ifach-
Benifallim
Sa de Aitana
Polop
La
Nucía
Altea
Ibi
Sella
Finestrat
Sierra Helada-
Sérra Gelada
astalla
Cuevas de Canalobre-
Coves de Canelobre
Benidorm
etrel-
etrer
Jijona-
Xixona
Busot
Villajoyosa-La Vila Joiosa
da
San Vicente del Raspeig-
Sant Vicent del Raspeig
El-Campello
ar-
er
San Juan de Alicante-
Sant Joan d'Alacant
Montforte del Cid-
Montforte del Sit
A7
ALICANTE-
ALACANT
Elche-
Elx
te-
t
Santa Pola
olores
moradí
Tabarca
Guardamar
del Segura
uel
as
Torrevieja
Campoamor-
Dehesa de Campoamor
an Pedro del Pinatar
vier
tiago de la Ribera
azares
or
La Manga
del Mar Menor
Cabo de Palos
Calblanque
e

0   10   20   30   40   50 km

COSTA BLANCA

D   E   F

Alicante &
Around

Alicante (Alacant), the provincial capital, is the Costa Blanca's main centre, a prosperous and bustling city in a fine coastal position, with interesting buildings, churches and museums, excellent restaurants, good shops and tourist facilities. For anyone on holiday in the region, Alicante is a must – a good contrast to days on the beach. Within easy reach are the historic cities of Elche (Elx) and Orihuela, both fascinating in their own way, the wine-growing area around Monóvar (Monòver), and a string of Moorish castles and small white towns. The scenery of the hinterland ranges from the mountains above the Vinalopó valley to the fertile plains, palm forests and salt flats behind the southern coast. Each of the seaside towns has its own character and charm, offering the essential holiday ingredients of sun, sand and sea.

> ' *Every day with perfect*
> *regularity a sky so blue that one*
> *can scoop it out with a spoon; a*
> *sun so glorious that the shadows*
> *are palpably black.* '
>
> HENRY ADAMS
> *Letter to*
> *Charles Milnes Gaskell* (1879)

Alicante (Alacant)

Curving round a bay and dominated by the ruins of its ancient castle, the city of Alicante, despite its thousands of foreign tourists, remains truly Spanish. It has everything you would expect of a Mediterranean city: a long and honourable history, venerable buildings, palm-lined avenues and seafront *paseos*, and all the amenities of a thriving modern provincial centre. The year-round mildness of the climate, sandy beaches and good hotels are added attractions for its many visitors.

The first settlement was established by the Greeks, who founded a colony they called Akra Leuka, the 'white headland', near modern Alicante. The Romans followed, founding their city of Lucentum, the City of Light. Like the rest of southern Spain, Alicante was invaded and settled by the Moors from the second half of the 8th century. For 500 years it was an Arab city and it was only in 1246 that Alfonso X regained it for the Castilian crown. In 1308 Alicante was incorporated into the kingdom of Valencia by Jaime III. Today it is the second largest city in Valencia and the capital of the fourth wealthiest province in Spain, its prosperity based on traditional and modern industry, agriculture and tourism. This stylish city has much to offer both residents and visitors; its festival of the Hogueras de San Juan is one of the most spectacular in Spain.

🛈 Rambla Méndez Núñez 23 ☎ 965 20 00 00; Plaza del Ayuntamiento 1 ☎ 900 21 10 27

🎟 Hogueras de San Juan (20–29 Jun); for additional festivals ► 116, or phone the tourist office

Below: *vivid tiles and paintwork complement traditional ironwork on old houses in Alicante*

Bottom: *a birds eye view of Alicante's marina and harbour*

What to See in Alicante

AYUNTAMIENTO ⭐

The twin-towered 18th-century town hall is one of Alicante's finest baroque buildings. An ornate doorway in the centre of the façade opens into a vast hall, from where an elegant stairway sweeps up to the state rooms and chapel on the first floor. Upstairs, the Salón Azul contains the city's earliest charter of privileges, and a small picture gallery. The lovely chapel is adorned with beautiful painted tiles, and over the altar hangs a painting of St Nicolás of Bari, the city's patron.

THE CENTRE ⭐

Alicante's centre consists of the old *barrios*, clustered at the foot of Monte Benecantil, and the broad avenues of the 19th-century city. Head for the Santa Cruz district (► 35), to find some of the city's oldest buildings, such as Museo de la Asegurada (a museum of 20th-century art), two 19th-century sanctuaries – and some great *tapas* bars.

Ramblas Méndez Núñez demarcates the 19th-century commercial centre, home to the colourful Mercado Central, one of the region's largest daily food markets. The main shopping area runs along the Avenida de Maisonnave and the streets around Avenida de Francisco Soto. This leads down to the Paseo de la Explanada de España, a lovely 19th-century palm-shaded walkway running parallel to the sea. Behind the Explanada lie the port and marina, an area well-served by terraced bars and cafes.

CONCATEDRAL DE SAN NICOLÁS DE BARI ⭐

In the heart of the oldest part of the city stands the cathedral, built between 1616 and 1662 to replace the 13th-century church that stood on the site of the city's mosque.

The tranquil cloisters of the cathedral of San Nicolás de Bari

The façade is simple Renaissance in style, but the interior, with its soaring dome, is much closer to baroque, heavy with carving and gilt. The 15th-century cloister, reached through a side door, provides an effective contrast.

✝ 33C4
✉ Plaza del Ayuntamiento 1
☎ 965 14 81 00
🕐 Mon–Fri 8–3
🚌 G, H, M
♿ Good
🎫 Free

✝ 33B4
🍴 Choice of restaurants and bars (€–€€€)
🚌 F, G, H, K, L, M

Museo de la Asegurada – Colección Arte Siglo XX
✝ 33C4
✉ Plaza de Santa María 3
☎ 965 14 07 68
🕐 Summer Tue–Sat 10–2, 5–9, Sun and hols 10:30–2:30; winter Tue–Sat 10–2, 4–8
♿ Good
🎫 Free

✝ 33B4
✉ Plaza Abad Penalva 1
☎ 965 21 26 62
🕐 Daily 7;30–12:30, 5:30–8
🍴 Restaurants/bars (€–€€€)
🚌 G, H, M
♿ Good
🎫 Free

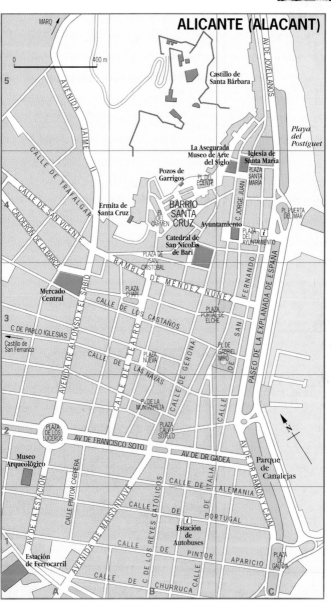

ALICANTE (ALACANT)

MARQ

0   400 m

Castillo de
Santa Bárbara

*Playa
del
Postiguet*

La Asegurada
Museo de Arte
del Siglo

Iglesia de
Santa María

Pozos de
Garrigos

PLAZA
SANTA
MARÍA

PL DEL
PUENTE

C/ JORGE JUAN

PL. PUERTA
DEL MAR

Ermita de
Santa Cruz

PL.
DEL
CARMEN

**BARRIO
SANTA
CRUZ**

Ayuntamiento

Catedral de
San Nicolás
de Bari

PLAZA
DEL
AYUNTAMIENTO

i

AVENIDA JAIME II

CALLE DE TRAFALGAR

CALLE DE SAN VICENTE

CALDERÓN DE LA BARCA

PLAZA DE
SAN
CRISTÓBAL

RAMBLA DE MÉNDEZ NÚÑEZ

FERNANDO

PASEO DE LA EXPLANADA DE ESPAÑA

AVENIDA DE LOVELLANOS

**Mercado
Central**

AVENIDA DE ALFONSO X EL SABIO

PLAZA
CHAPÍ

CALLE DE LOS CASTAÑOS

PLAZA
PORTAL DE
ELCHE

SAN

C DE PABLO IGLESIAS

Castillo de
San Fernando

CALLE DE

CALLE DEL TEATRO

PLAZA
NUEVA

LAS NAVAS

CALLE DE GERONA

PL DE
GABRIEL
MIRÓ

DE

CALLE

PL DE LA
MONTAÑETA

PLAZA
CALVO
SOTELO

N

PLAZA
DE LOS
LUCEROS

AV DE FRANCISCO SOTO

AV DE DR GADEA

AVDE DR RAMÓN Y CAJAL

*Parque
de
Canalejas*

**Museo
Arqueológico**

AV DE LA ESTACIÓN

CALLE PINTOR CABRERA

AVENIDA DE MAISONNAVE

CALLE DE LOS REYES CATÓLICOS

CALLE DE ITALIA

CALLE DE ALEMANIA

CALLE DE PORTUGAL

CALLE DE

i

**Estación
de
Autobuses**

CALLE

PINTOR

APARICIO

PLAZA
DE
GALICIA

**Estación
de Ferrocarril**

CALLE DE

C CHURRUCA

A   B   C

33C4
Plaza de Santa Maria
965 21 60 26
Daily 9:30–1, 6:30–8:30
Choice of restaurants and bars near by
G, H, M, P, S
Few   Free

33A2
Plaza Dr Gómez Ulla s/n
965 14 90 00
Tue–Sat, 10–2, 4–8; Sun 10–2
2, 6, 9, 20, 23
Albufereta and San Juan served by Alicante–Dénia line
Excellent
Moderate
Castillo de Santa Bárbara (► 17)

Bars at all locations (€)
All served by city buses
All good
All free

Stroll in the shade of the palms on the waterfront Explanada de España

IGLESIA DE SANTA MARÍA

Alicante's oldest church was built in the 13th century on the site of a mosque in the heart of the original Arab town. It has been frequently altered and is today a marvellous *mélange* of different architectural styles. The baroque doorway leads into a nave which is an outstanding example of Valencian Gothic. The great golden altar dates from the late 1400s and the font from the following century.

MARQ (MUSEO ARQUEOLÓGICO PROVINCIAL DE ALICANTE)

Selling itself as the 21st century's first archeological museum, MARQ is a superb example of how to bring ancient history alive. Its four main galleries are crammed with artefacts and treasures focusing respectively on prehistory, the Iberian civilisation, the Romans and the Middle Ages. But the exhibits are only one part of the whole experience, and most visitors will be as, or more, fascinated by the state-of-the-art visual, light and sound effects. Videos show ancient man tool-making and throwing pots, computer graphics bring the Roman past to life around the visitor, Arab and medieval music echo through the galleries, and the excellent lighting system adds drama everywhere. If you thought archeology was dull, MARQ may help you change your mind.

PARKS

Alicante has two major parks, the Parque Tossal, near the the city's other castle, San Fernando, and El Palmeral, on the southern outskirts. Both are laid out with palms, trees and exotic plants and have good facilities for children.

Around Alicante

Start at the east end of the tree-lined, tesselated Explanada de España (▶ 34) and cut north for two blocks into the Plaza del Ayuntamiento, to emerge opposite the town hall (▶ 32), with its marvellous façade and twin towers. Turn right along the Calle de Jorge Juan then left up the steps to the Plaza de Santa María.

The lovely Gothic church (▶ 34) is finely balanced by the Museo de la Asegurada (▶ 32).

Take the steps up the narrow Calle Instituto, by the museum, and turn left into Plaça del Pont, the site of the Pozos de Garrigos, underground water tanks. Follow the Calle de Toledo left out of the plaza until you reach the Plaza del Carmen.

This is the heart of the Barrio Santa Cruz, the oldest part of Alicante.

Cross the square and take Carrer San Rafael, right, up steps. Near the top turn left into Carrer de Sant Antoni, then right up Calle Dipurado Auset (sign to Ermita de Santa Cruz) up more steps.

Here is the Ermita de Santa Cruz, a 19th-century shrine lying just below the Torreón de la Ampollo, one of old wall's surviving towers.

Walk back along San Antoni and turn right down the steps, then left down San Rafael to return to Plaza del Carmen. Cross the square and continue down Carrer de Argensola to Plaza de San Cristóbal, where you turn left down Calle Labradores, lined with 18th-century houses and leading to San Nicolás cathedral (▶ 32). Head west along the Calle de Miguel Soler to Rambla de Méndez Núñez, where you turn left towards the sea. A left turn at the bottom brings you back to the Explanada de España.

Distance
2km

Time
2–3 hours, depending on visits

Start/end point
Explanada de España

🔲 33C3

🚌 S, G, M

Lunch
Darsena (€€)

✉ Muella de Levant 6, Marina Deportiva

☎ 965 20 75 89

The shrine of the Ermita de Santa Cruz in Alicante's oldest quarter attracts many local pilgrims

What to See Around Alicante

AGRES ⊕

🕀 29D5
✉ 65km northwest of Alicante
🍴 Restaurants/bars (€–€€)
🚌 From Alicante and Alcoy
ℹ Ayuntamiento de Agres, ☎ 965 51 00 01
❓ Mare de Deu de Agres (1–9 Sep); San Miguel (29 Sep)

Tucked in the northern inland corner of Alicante (Alacant) province, Agres is a quiet upland agricultural village, set around an ancient convent and a castle. It makes a good jumping-off point for exploring the Sierra de Mariola, the Gallinera valley (▶ 18–19), and inland towns such as Alcoy (▶ 36) and Biar (▶ 37). The surrounding hills are wonderful walking country, carpeted with wild herbs and dotted with *pozos de nieve*, medieval ice-houses.

Above: *looking across the gorge to the centre of Alcoy*
Inset: *pigeons strutting on the expanse of the Plaza de Dins, Alcoy*

ALCOY (ALCOI) ⊕

🕀 29D4
✉ 48km northwest of Alicante
🍴 Choice of restaurants and bars (€–€€€)
🚌 From Alicante
🚍 From Alicante
♿ Few
ℹ San Lorenzo 2 ☎ 965 53 71 55
❓ Moros y Cristianos (22–24 Apr)
↔ Agres (▶ 36), Biar (▶ 37)

Modern Alcoy stands on a promontory, first settled by the Iberians, between the rivers Molonar and Barchell, its houses tumbling down the sides of a gorge. It's the largest industrial centre in the area, a solid, prosperous and seemingly dour town, worth seeing for its position and fine 19th-century architecture. Centred around the grandiose Plaza de España (Plaça d'Espanya) and the arcaded Plaza de Dins (Plaça de Dins), Alcoy is scattered with baroque churches and civic buildings, dating mainly from the end of the 19th century. The money came from cotton, still processed here, and was spent on extending the 17th-century city, and building the five bridges across the gorge.

The town has the fascinating **Museo de Fiestas** where the costumes used in the Moros y Christianos festival are stored. This rumbustious event celebrates a Christian victory over the Moors in 1279, when Saint George came to the aid of the inhabitants, and is a source of huge local pride. The Museu Arqueológico Municipal has a good local collection, which includes some Iberian treasures.

Museo de Fiestas
- ✉ San Miguel 60
- ⏰ Tue–Fri 11:30–1:30, 5:30–7:30, Sat, Sun 11:30–1:30
- ♿ Few
- 🎫 Inexpensive

BIAR ✪

Steeped in history and dominated by its Moorish castle, Biar is one of the most attractive of the ancient valley towns that once guarded the Castilian border. The town, a Moorish stronghold, was taken by Castile but fell to Aragon in 1245 and became an important frontier post. Today Biar is a charming town, and it is worth spending time wandering about and soaking up the atmosphere. Steep and narrow streets and peaceful plazas lead up to the fortress, with its solid walls and magnificent free-standing Moorish tower. There are fine valley views from the **Castillo de Biar** and an interesting Gothic church with later additions and a superb plateresque doorway.

- ✚ 29D4
- ✉ 55km west of Alicante
- 🍴 Restaurants/bars (€–€€)
- 🚌 From Alicante
- ℹ Avenida de Villena 2
  ☎ 965 81 11 77
- ♿ Few
- ❓ Moros y Cristianos (10–13 May)
- ↔ Agres, Alcoy (▶ 36)

Castillo de Biar
- ☎ 965 81 03 74 for opening times and key

CUEVAS DE CANALOBRE (COVES DE CANELOBRE) ✪

The hills of Cabeçó d'Or, north of Alicante, are riddled with caves and grottoes. This impressive limestone cavern, with one of the highest vaults in Spain, has been skilfully illuminated to show off the stalactites, stalagmites and strange limestone formations. Among the many odd shapes is one known as the *canalobre*, candelabra, from which the cave gets its name.

- ✚ 29D4
- ✉ 24km north of Alicante and 40km southwest of Benidorm
- ☎ 965 69 92 50
- ⏰ 20 Jun–1 Oct daily 10:30–7:50; 2 Oct–19 Jun daily 11–5:50
- 🍴 Restaurant and bar (€–€€)
- ♿ Few
- ❓ Concerts are sometimes held in the caves in summer; details from local tourist offices
- ↔ Alicante (▶ 30–5), Villajoyosa (▶ 75)

The stalactites in the Cuevas de Canalobre – a popular local attraction

37

The blue-domed basilica of Santa María stands at the heart of old Elche

ELCHE (ELX) ⭐⭐

Surrounded and infiltrated by Europe's largest palm forest, the ancient city of Elche stands on the Vinalopó river. Spain's shoe-manufacturing capital, Elche is a stronghold of the Valencian language and one of the most historic towns in the region. Founded as an Iberian settlement named Illici, the Romans called it Iulia Illice Augusta. It became an important Visigothic episcopal centre, served as a major Moorish power base, was retaken by Jaime I in 1265 and has since quietly prospered. The old town, on the east bank of the river, contains almost everything worth seeing, so visitors can ignore the modern town, though some of the shoe factory outlets are worth visiting.

More than 300,000 palms grow in Elche, in verdant parks and shady squares and lining streets and gardens (▶ 21). The groves probably originated in Phoenician times and are protected by law. Many trees bear dates, and these are often for sale from street vendors. A miniature train tours the larger groves several times a day, or you can hire a bicycle and follow a mapped route through some of the plantations around the city's edge.

Elche's main sights are clustered around the vast baroque basilica of Santa María, whose blue-tiled dome dominates the ancient town centre. Built in the 16th and 17th centuries, the basilica, dark and cavernous inside and a mass of exuberant carving outside, is the scene in August of Elche's fiesta, the Misteri d'Elx. This medieval mystery play, celebrating in words and haunting music the death and assumption of the Virgin, has probably been performed by the townspeople since the 1260s, soon after the Reconquest. You can learn more about this at the **Museu Municipal de la Festa**, where the excellent audio-visual show gives some idea of the drama and beauty of the festival for which Elche is renowned.

Near the cathedral, Elche's **Museo Arqueológico** is housed in the Palacio Altamira. The collection includes some wonderful Iberian pottery and stone pieces from the more important Museo Monográfico de Alcudia. This stands on the site of Illici, considered to be one of Spain's most important Iberian centres, a short distance outside Elche. The town centre has some fine Moorish remains. The Calaforra, or watchtower, is a remarkably complete building that has an extraordinary *mudéjar* hallway, while near by, the 15th-century Renaissance façade of the **Convento de la Mercé** fronts a serene cloister and a set of Arab baths.

From the centre of the city a pleasant stroll leads through the old Moorish quarter of Raval to the Franciscan monastery church of San José, where you can see *azejulos*, frescoes and carvings.

Museo Arqueológico Altamira
☎ 965 45 36 03
🕐 Tue–Sat 10–1, 4–7, Sun 10–1
♿ Good 💰 Inexpensive

Convento de la Mercé
🕐 Tue–Sat 10–1, 4:30–8:30, Sun 10–1
♿ Good 💰 Free

Freshly cut branches from Elche's palm forest are carried in procession on Palm Sunday

Elche is particularly noted for its festivals. Besides La Festa in August, Palm Sunday is a major celebration, with thousands of people, all dressed in new clothes, processing with palm branches through the palm trees themselves. Late December sees the Vinguda de la Mare de Déu, a procession from the sea to Elche, commemorating the legendary arrival of the text of the mystery play.

Did you know ?

In the palm groves in and around Elche you'll see some trees with their fronds tied together in bundles; this is to bleach the branches, which are then made into the palm crosses distributed in churches all over Europe for Palm Sunday.

Food & Drink

The cooking of this part of Spain has a robust style all of its own, using the freshest seafood, locally raised meat and lots of fruit and vegetables; the classic *montaña y mar* combination of the coastal regions of Spain.

Below: *fresh shellfish, ready to be cooked to order*
Bottom: *newly picked olives ready for pressing*
Right: *world-renowned paella valenciana*

Mar y Tierra

Rice is the culinary king: *paella valenciana* springs to mind at once, but much more typical are dishes such as *arroz abanda* and *caldera* on the coast, *arroz con costra* and *paella huertanos* on the plains, and *arroces serranos* in the hills. These truly local dishes combine rice with tiny fish, with pork and vegetables, and with game and wild herbs. Traditionally only part of a meal, these are followed by fish dishes, robust stews or spit-roasted meat. Look out for *gazpacho de mero*, a fish stew served with flatbread, grilled *emparador* and *lenguado*, swordfish and sole, and large, whole fish baked in a salt crust – *dorada al sal*. Succulent *cochinillo*, suckling pig, the inland *gazpachos*, highly spiced meat stews eaten with flatbread, or *trigo picado*, a traditional cracked wheat dish, are all excellent. Winter country stews include *olleta* and

giraboix, based on dried beans and meats cooked with mountain herbs and saffron. In Murcia the freshness of the local produce spills over into the cooking: green garlic and sweet *pimentón* flavour dishes inspired by the huge range of fruit and vegetables.

Desserts & Sweets

Local oranges, lemons, peaches, cherries and other fruit appear alongside the ubiquitous *flan* (caramel custard), and feature in tarts and as glacé fruits. Almonds are everywhere; popular in ultra-sweet Moorish-inspired biscuits, sumptuous puddings and cakes, often flavoured with local honey. Sampling *turrón* – a nougat sweetmeat traditionally eaten at Christmas – is a must.

Snacks

Main meals apart, there is still plenty to try. *Tapas*, the small platefuls of food served with drinks, can easily substitute for lunch or dinner. Fish, shellfish, olives, slices of ham and sausage, vegetable specialities and local almonds are just a few of the everyday offerings in many bars. Just point and ask for a *porción* or a *ración*. Do as many natives do and have breakfast out – what could be more heavenly than *churros*, the long sugar-dusted fritters, dipped into a steaming cup of coffee or thick hot chocolate?

Thirst-quenchers & Wines

The Costa Blanca produces some excellent wines from the main areas of Monóvar (Monòver) and Jumilla – the red from the latter region with an astonishing 18 per cent alcohol content. Monóvar makes deep reds and delicate rosés as well as a famous dessert wine, Fondillón. The lesser-known Pinosa and Ricote wines are good and moscatel is the region's distinctive dessert wine. Alicante has its own herbal digestive, Cantueso. *Sangría*, *cava*, fresh orange juice, *horchata* – a nut-milk drink made from almonds or tiger nuts – and *granizada*, a fruit slush, will all slip down well at different times of the day.

Top: *locally grown fruit and vegetables go straight from the market to the table*

Above: Sangría – *red wine and fruit make this the perfect summer evening drink*

🔲 29D3

✉️ 40km south of Alicante

🍴 Restaurants and bars
(€–€€€)

🚢 To Isla de Tabarca,
Cruceros Tabarda

☎️ 966 70 21 22

ℹ️ Plaza de la Constitución 7

☎️ 965 72 72 92

♿ Few

❓ Contact tourist office for
festival information

↔️ Elche (➤ 38)

**Museo Arqueológico y
Etnológico**

✉️ Casa de Cultura, Colón 60

🕐 Apr–Oct 10–2, 5–7.
Closed Sun

💶 Inexpensive ♿ Few

🔲 29D4

✉️ 22km north of Alicante

🍴 Restaurants/bars (€–€€€)

🚌 Bus from Alicante

♿ Few

Turrones el Lobo

✉️ Alcoy 62

🕐 Mon–Sat 10–1:30, 4–6:30

Above: *these picturesque
old beachside houses at
Guardamar have
absorbed years of salt,
sun and wind*

42

GUARDAMAR DEL SEGURA

Surrounded by citrus fruit orchards and fertile vegetable gardens, the ancient settlement of Guardamar, at the mouth of the Segura river, is a thriving small town and summer resort. Inhabited first by the Iberians at their settlement of Cabero Lucero, the area was occupied by the Romans before becoming a major Moorish religious centre, known as Rábita Califal. The Christians ousted the Moors in the 13th century, built a castle and a church, and the village developed into a fishing and agricultural centre, its peace only disturbed by an 1829 earthquake, when it was rebuilt further away from the river. Guardamar is surrounded by the Dunas, rolling sand dunes planted with eucalyptus, palms and pines, making its beaches some of the loveliest on the coast (➤ 82–3). The spring and summer see a string of festivals; you can learn more local history at the **Museo Arqueológico y Etnológico**, and there is a lively market each Wednesday.

JIJONA (XIXONA)

Jijona, in the sierras behind Alicante (Alacant), is a mecca for the sweet-toothed. This everyday little town, with its old castle and narrow streets, is the home of *turrón,* an almond and honey-based nougat traditionally eaten at Christmastime.

Probably of Moorish origin, its manufacture has a long history in Jijona and it is still produced by over 30 small-scale family businesses on an artisan basis, with many of the production processes done by hand. It comes in a bewildering variety, ranging from soft and gooey through slightly crisp to tooth-cracking caramel, studded with glistening almonds. You can visit one of the genuine family businesses and there is a small museum, **Turrones el Lobo**, devoted to ancient production methods.

MONÓVAR (MONÒVER) ✪

A visit to this thriving little town, rising from a green sea of rolling vineyards, is a must for wine-lovers. The 19th century saw the strong, slightly sweet Monóvar reds fetching astronomical prices after phylloxera destroyed the French vineyards. Monastrel grapes are used for the reds, whose depth and strength comes from the *doble pasta* production method, where a first batch of grapes and must is mixed with a second one in the same vat before fermentation begins. The excellent and delicate rosés owe their bouquet to another local method, where the wine is fermented from must drawn off from a first light crushing of the grapes. Sample, too, the perfumed and aromatic sweet dessert wine Fondillón, which needs 20 years to mature. Traditional vineyard tools and implements are on show in the idiosyncratic **Museo de Artes y Oficios**. Wine-tasting is available at Bodega Salvador Poveda.

- 🚑 29D4
- ✉ 40km west of Alicante
- 🍴 Choice of restaurants and bars (€–€€€)
- 🚌 Bus from Alicante
- ♿ Few
- ↔ Sax (➤ 48)

Museo de Artes y Oficios

- ✉ Rondo de la Constitución 11
- ☎ 965 47 02 70 to arrange a visit

A vineyard worker in Monóvar's wine country

NOVELDA ✪

The town of Novelda, approached through a fertile valley planted with vines and almonds, was one of the string of important Moorish fortress towns lining the inland valleys. Outside the town rises the Castillo de la Mola, whose superb 14th-century triangular tower was designed by Ibrahim of Tunis; stretches of ancient walling still stand. Just below is the sanctuary of Santa Magdalena, a Gaudí-influenced church by Sala, a local architect and engineer. There are some other interesting buildings in town, including some fine Modernist houses, one of which, La Casa Modernista, at Mayor 24, contains the local museum.

- 🚑 29D3
- ✉ 30km west of Alicante
- 🍴 Choice of restaurants and bars (€–€€€)
- 🚌 Bus from Alicante
- ❓ Moros y Cristianos (19–25 Jul); Santa Magdalena (20 Jul and 7 Aug)
- ↔ Monóvar (➤ 43), Sax (➤ 48)

Orihuela

The ancient town of Orihuela makes a good target if you are aiming for a genuine historic inland town, unswamped by tourists, with a mix of impressive monuments, crumbling palaces and a gentle pace of life. Easily reached from the coast, a visit here could be combined with a trip to Elche (Elx, ➤ 38) for a taste of untouched provincial Spain.

Called Aurariola by the Romans, the town stands in the lower reaches of the wonderfully fertile Segura valley, approached through a stately palm forest, Spain's second largest. From here, Ferdinand and Isabella embarked on the final push for Granada. Later, the town became a wealthy Renaissance cathedral and university city, the commercial focus for the surrounding area. In the 19th century, a combination of Alicante's (Alacant's) new role as regional capital and a destructive earthquake diminished Orihuela's importance. Today the old churches, theatre, palaces and restored historic centre provide a backdrop to the everyday life of this prosperous inland town.

✚ 28C3

✉ 60km southwest of Alicante

🍴 Choice of restaurants and bars

🚌 From Alicante

🚊 From Alicante

ℹ Palacio Rubalcava, Francisco Diez 25

☎ 965 30 27 47

🎉 Semana Santa (Mar/Apr); Moros y Cristianos (17 Jul); Virgen de Monserrat (8 Sep)

↔ Elche (➤ 38)

Graceful vaulting rises above the main altar in Orihuela's cathedral

What to See in Orihuela

LA CATEDRAL ✪✪

This cathedral, with its nearby 18th-century bishop's palace, started life as a simple church, built between 1305 and 1355. Over the centuries alterations and additions have produced a wonderful mixture of styles, ranging from Romanesque through Catalan Gothic to baroque. The vaulted transept, built in 1500, is a high point, its bizarre, spirally twisted ribs rising to the shadows of the roof. More embellishments followed after the church became a cathedral in 1564; these include a richly carved choir, an ornate baroque organ and a couple of ambulatory chapels. The serene two-storey cloister, its honey-coloured arches enclosing a trim garden, was moved here after the Civil War. It contains the **Museo Diocesano del Arte Sacro**, a surprisingly rich collection which includes a Velázquez masterpiece, *The Temptation of St Thomas*.

✉ Plaza Teniente Linares s/n

🕐 Mon–Fri 10:30–1:30, 5:30–7:30, Sat 10:30–1:30

✋ Free ♿ Good

Museo Diocesano del Arte Sacro

🕐 Mon–Fri 10:30–1:30, 4–6.30, Sat 10:30–1:30, 5–7:30

✋ Inexpensive

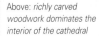

Above: *richly carved woodwork dominates the interior of the cathedral*

45

Right: *encircling steep hillsides provide the background for Orihuela and its palm groves*

Opposite: *the flamboyant stone doorway at Santo Domingo – one of Orihuela's artistic treasures*

COLEGIO DE SANTO DOMINGO ✪✪

Founded as a Dominican monastery and now a private school, Santo Domingo's architectural heyday coincided with its later role, from 1569 to 1824, as a university. During this time the three superb doorways were added to the main façade, and the elegant cloistered patios and sweeping panelled main staircase were built. Don't miss the refectory – its stunning *azulejo* frieze is one of the finest examples of this beautiful tile-work to be seen in this part of Spain.

✉ Francisco Die
🕐 Mon–Fri 10:30–1:30, 5:30–7:30, Sat 10:30–1:30
♿ Good
🎟 Free

IGLESIA DE SANTIAGO ✪

This lovely Catalan Gothic church has a fine Isabelline-style front, the Puerto de Santiago, and a severe 16th-century nave and transept, dramatically punctuated by the opulence of the baroque Capilla Mayor and Salzillo's lyrical altarpieces.

✉ Plaza de la Merced 1
🕐 Mon–Fri 10:30–1:30, 5:30–7:30, Sat 10:30–1:30
♿ Few
🎟 Inexpensive

MUSEO SEMANA SANTA ✪

A visit here will help explain the tremendous impact that Holy Week has in Spain even today. The museum houses a collection of the massive carved floats, many by Salzillo, used in the processions held during the week before Easter. The ghastly figure known as the *Paso de la Diablesa*, the She-Devil, and her skeleton companion, have been encouraging sinners to repent since 1688, when Nicolás de Busi created them.

✉ Santa Justa
🕐 Mon–Fri 10:30–1:30, 5:30–7:30, Sat 10:30–1:30
♿ Good
🎟 Free

SANTAS JUSTA Y RUFINA ✪

Near the splendid Renaissance town hall stands the austere and serene 14th-century church of Saints Justa and Rufina. Its gargoyled clock tower, the most southerly example of Catalan Gothic architecture, is one of the oldest buildings in Orihuela.

✉ Clavarana
🕐 Mon–Fri 10:30–1:30, 4–7
♿ Few
🎟 Inexpensive

SEMINARIO DE SAN MIGUEL ✪

The old Seminario de San Miguel stands on the slopes of a hill above the town. It's worth the climb for the tranquillity and good views of the town and fertile plain, and a glimpse of the ruined castle above.

✉ Uphill from Plaza Caturia
🕐 Not open to the public
♿ None

SANTA POLA ✪

✚ 29D3
✉ 18km south of Alicante
🍴 Restaurants/bars (€–€€€)
🚌 From Alicante
⛴ To Isla de Tabarca; daily in summer, Cruceros Tabardo ☎ 966 70 21 22 or Barco Santa Pola ☎ 965 41 11 13
ℹ Plaza Diputación s/n ☎ 966 69 22 76
♿ Few
❓ Moros y Cristianos (1–8 Sep)
↔ Elche (➤ 38)

Acuario Municipal
✉ Plaza Fernández Ordoñez
☎ 966 69 15 32
🕐 Mon–Fri 10–2, 5–7:30, Sat, Sun 10:30–2
♿ Few
💰 Inexpensive

Santa Pola functions successfully both as the home of a huge Mediterranean fishing fleet and as a lively resort, with good sporting facilities, some attractive buildings and a vibrant street market. South of the town stretch miles of smooth, clean sandy beaches backed by pines and eucalyptus. Behind these beaches the salt flats are a designated natural park, where you can spot flamingoes and a wide variety of birds of passage, as well as a range of coastal flora. The town's fortress and two rather dilapidated watchtowers date from the mid-16th century, when fear of Berber pirate raids was high; the fortress now houses the town's cultural centre and the Museo del Mar, with displays on the coast and sea. The other attraction is the **Acuario Municipal** (aquarium), its tanks holding a variety of fish and sea creatures. An audio-visual theatre features presentations on conservation which is fast becoming a priority along the coast. Well worth a visit for the daily afternoon fish market and for its agreeable summer street life, Santa Pola offers pavement cafés and a good range of excellent fish restaurants.

SAX ✪

✚ 29D4
✉ 45km west of Alicante
🍴 Restaurant/bars (€–€€)
🚌 From Alicante
🚆 From Alicante
♿ Few
❓ Moros y Cristianos (1–5 February); San Pancracio (1 May)
↔ Biar (➤ 37), Villena (➤ 53)

Castillo de Sax
☎ 965 47 40 06 for opening times and key

The town of Sax, spreading down the hillside of the Vinalopó valley (➤ 53), is one of a picturesque chain of settlements dominated by castles, and is a good stopping point. The **Castillo de Sax** takes full advantage of its natural surroundings, the line of its walls following the contours of the limestone ridge on which it is built. The Moors first built a fortress here in the 10th century. The 12th-century Levante tower survives from this era but the two courtyards and fine three-storey keep are later. Sax, despite its superb defensive position, was finally taken by the Christians in the late 13th century. It then became part of the Marquisate of Villena until absorbed into the kingdom of Ferdinand and Isabella. The town's small Museo Arqueológico (archaeological museum) helps put this fascinating area into perspective.

Guadalest & the Sierra de Aitana

Take the E15 motorway north from Alicante and exit on to the C3318 (70) running inland to Callosa de Ensarriá. Continue on this road to visit the Fonts del Algar (➤ 65). Cut back to Callosa and take the C3313 (755) into the hills.

As the road climbs, terraces first levelled in Moorish times and washed with the pink of almond blossom in February, cling to the lower slopes. The road rises steadily until a sharp corner brings Guadalest (➤ 20) into view.

After visiting the village and its castle, continue upwards past the white villages of Benimantell and Confrides to cross the pass of Puerto de Ares.

As you lose height, the vegetation changes and pines and olives dot the terraces and hillside.

Through Ares village turn left on to the A170 and past Alcolecha.

The country here in the superb landscape of the Sierra de Aitana is much wilder, scattered with pines, juniper and a plethora of wild herbs and aromatic shrubs.

After 9km take the left fork on to the A173 to Sella, passing the Safari Aitana wildlife park (➤ 111).

The upland scenery, with the ochre-coloured peak of Aitana (1,558m) surging up from the valley, gives way gradually to impeccably kept terracing once more, orange and almond trees are underplanted with vegetables and salad plants.

Drive through Sella and after 6km take a left turn on to the A1741 to Finestrat, and then the A1735 to return to Benidorm, Alicante and the coast.

Distance
122km

Time
3 hours without stops or most of a day with visits

Start/end point
Alicante
✚ 29D3

Lunch
La Fonda
✉ Carretera Alcoy 15, Sella
☎ 965 87 90 11

Left: *workaday fishing boats harboured on Santa Pola's waterfront*

Below: *vivid green almond trees in a well-tended orchard*

In the Know

If you only have a short time to visit Costa Blanca, or would like to get a real flavour of the region, here are some ideas:

10
Ways to Be a Local

Blend in by behaving like the locals, and don't wear inappropriate clothes away from the beach. Spaniards are clean and smart in towns and restaurants.

Try to speak Spanish – even a few basic phrases will be appreciated and will make you feel part of the place.

Shake hands and smile. Spanish manners are formal and a smile will win friends even if you don't speak Spanish.

Eat late – away from the coast meal times are late; lunch at around 2 and dinner well after 8.

Don't get drunk – it's the worst social crime in the book and cancels all previous goodwill you've gained.

Exchanging local news in Alicante

Have a siesta and then enjoy staying up really late into the balmy summer nights.

Taking an early evening stroll before dinner is the time to wear your smart outfits, window-shop and have an aperitif at a pavement café.

Show respect in churches and cathedrals; Spain is still a religious country.

Don't be judgemental about Spain, its people or politics; leave that to the natives, it's their country.

Be an adventurous eater – there are local specialities everywhere, so try them.

10
Good Places to Have Lunch

El Cantó (€) Calle de Alemania 26, Alicante ☎ 965 92 56 50. One of Alicante's best bets for a quick and delicious lunch, El Cantó is always packed with Spaniards.

Los Charros (€€) ✉ Avenida de Bruselas 10, Playa de San Juan ☎ 965 16 00 82. Traditional cooking and a huge selection of the best *tapas* near this beach.

El Cranc (€) ✉ Playa de l'Olla, Altea ☎ 965 84 19 46. A friendly and relaxed place to have lunch near the beach with a huge range of *tapas*.

L'Obrer (€€) ✉ Carretera de Benimantell 27, Guadalest ☎ 965 88 50 88. Popular tourist restaurant with a terrace serving traditional mountain dishes and grilled meat.

El Rincón de las Jarres (€€) ✉ María Parodi 3, Torrevieja ☎ 965 71 09 60. Seafood and country dishes are the specialities in this lively bar-cum-restaurant.

Ca L'Angeles (€€) ✉ Gabriel Miró 36, Polop ☎ 965 87 02 26. Good country cooking with many traditional dishes in a

pleasantly converted old building.

Altamar (€€) ✉ Jaime I 96, Playa de Muchavista, El Campello ☎ 965 65 66 33. Restaurant right on the beach with a good bar and terrace and a great range of rice dishes.

Sota (€) ✉ Canovas del Castillo 56, Jumilla ☎ 968 78 03 24. A good bar for a quick and delicious lunch from the range of interesting *tapas*.

Casa Enrique (€) ✉ Empedra 10, Elche (Elx) ☎ 965 45 15 77. Friendly local place with a bar and restaurant serving excellent *arroz con costra* (➤ 40).

El Pegolí (€€) ✉ Punta de Palos 103, Les Rotes 96, Dénia ☎ 965 78 10 35. Restaurant outside town specialising in seafood and shellfish of all kinds.

Top Activities

Swimming in hotel pools, off sandy beaches and from rocks into deep water. Head for the Blue Flag beaches for high standards of upkeep and facilities.

Sailing – if you haven't tried it before, now's your chance at one of the many sailing schools up and down the coast.

Windsurfing – available through hotels and clubs; the Mar Menor is a good place to try if you're a novice.

Golf – there are more than 20 quality courses in the area, most with equipment for hire.

Tennis – there are clubs at all the resorts and many hotels have their own courts.

Walking – get away from the crowds along the coast and explore the superb inland sierras.

Scuba diving – explore the underwater riches of the coast; Calpe (Calp), Isla de Tabarca and Mazarrón are good areas.

Riding – experience the peace of the countryside on horseback.

Hot-air ballooning – glide silently over the palm forest of Elche.

Cycling – hire a bicycle to get around your resort and further afield.

Top Views

- Jávea (Xàbia) and its bay from the Cabo de San Antonio.
- South down the coast from Cabo de la Nao (Cap de la Nau).
- The Guadalest valley from the terrace below the Castillo de Guadalest.
- The view to the hills and coast from the Coll de Rates.
- The Peñón de Ifach from above Calpe (Calp).
- Alicante and the coast from the Castillo de Santa Bárbara.
- The Sierra de Espuña from the pine woods of the natural park.
- Benidorm at night from La Cala or the Punta de la Escaleta.
- The Gallinera valley from the Planes road.
- Castillo de Játiva from below, and the views from the Castillo to the town.

Traditionally shaped and patterned handmade ceramics are a lasting souvenir

Souvenir Ideas

Ceramics and pottery, from cheerful hand-painted bowls and plates to a delicate Lladro figure.

Cane and basketware from Gata de Gorgos; baskets, trays, esparto mats, chairs or tables.

Shoes and bags – locally produced soft, comfortable footwear and elegant bags make an excellent buy.

Strings of dried garlic and peppers to brighten your kitchen and pep up your cooking.

Belén figures – the intricate and delicate traditional figures used in Christmas cribs.

Cotton goods – Spanish cotton is excellent quality.

Paella pans – the best place to buy the real thing is a local street market.

Almonds – plain, roast or salted, are top quality and grown in the hills of the region.

Turrón – almost all of the traditional Christmas nougat is produced in the Costa Blanca.

Local wines and liqueurs – to remind you of visits to vineyards and atmospheric *bodegas*.

TABARCA ⚹⚹

➕ 29D3

✉ 15km south of Alicante

🍴 Restaurants (€€–€€€)

🚢 From Alicante, Cruceros Kon Tiki ☎ 966 08 21 18; from Santa Pola, Cruceros Baeza-Paradi ☎ 965 41 23 38; from Guardamar, Cruceros Tabarca ☎ 966 70 21 22; from Torrevieja, Cruceros Tabarca ☎ 966 70 21 22

♿ Few

🏢 Guardamar del Segura (➤ 42)

Boats run from several coastal towns to the Islote de la Cantera, a small group of islands where breezes blow even on the hottest days and the crystal-clear waters tempt snorkellers and divers. The main island is Tabarca, fortified and settled by Carlos III in the 18th century as a prison island for Genoese captives. The original walled town survives, with its stately entrance gate and church, but most summer visitors come here for the beaches, swimming and wonderful fish restaurants. The waters round the archipelago are a designated marine reserve, with some of the most interesting underwater life along the whole of the Costa Blanca. The shore base is in the old lighthouse, which you can visit on an island walk. It's best in the late afternoon when most visitors have gone.

TORREVIEJA ⚹

➕ 29D2

✉ 48km south of Alicante

🍴 Restaurants/bars (€–€€€)

🚌 From Alicante

🚆 From Alicante via Elche

🚢 To Isla de Tauarca, Cruceros Tabarca ☎ 966 70 21 22

ℹ Plaza Ruiz Capdepont s/n ☎ 965 70 34 33

♿ Few

❓ Real de la Feria (May), Virgen del Carmen (16 Jul)

🏢 Guardamar del Segura (➤ 42)

Torrevieja's distinctive low-level houses and wide streets date from its rebuilding after a catastrophic earthquake, though older buildings survive, including the remains of the Roman port. With its beaches, sports facilities, Museo de la Semana Santa, restaurants and summer nightlife, the town is a popular holiday centre. Spanish music fans flock here in August for the Habanera Festival, a celebration of the lilting songs brought back to the town from Cuba by the 19th-century salt exporters. Torrevieja's salt flats are Europe's oldest and largest, sparkling flat expanses where salt water evaporates to produce pure sea salt, still widely exported. The salt flats at Torrevieja and La Mata are now also designated natural parks and have more than 250 recorded species of birds feeding on them. Find out more at the Museo del Mar y Sal.

VILLENA ⭐

This lively little town, lying in the wine-producing area of the Vinalopó valley, is dominated by La Atalaya, the water tower, a square-towered 15th-century castle. The original fortress was built by the Moors as one of a chain running up the valley, but Villena's history predates the Arabs by thousands of years. The **Museo Arqueológico**, housed in the lovely 1707 town hall, has collections spanning 8,000 years of early local history. The star attraction is the extraordinary gold hoard discovered near by in the 1960s, whose solid gold pots, bowls, necklaces and bracelets date from around 3000 BC. Other treasures, including more gold, come from various nearby sites including the Bronze Age capital of the area, Cabeza Redonda. Villena's 16th-century church of Santiago, with its tapering barley-sugar columns soaring up to shadowy vaulting, is a must for Levantine Gothic enthusiasts. The wonderfully ornate font was carved by Jacopo Fiorentino, an assistant of Michelangelo, who settled in Villena.

VINALOPÓ VALLEY ⭐

The Vinalopó river gives its name to a broad valley running southwest from the hill country behind Alicante's coastline to the plains. For centuries a strategic route, the valley was frontier territory for Carthaginians and Romans, Moors and Christians, and the rising new powers of Castile and Aragon in the years following the Reconquest. A chain of defensive castles, some wonderfully complete, testifies to these times and a drive up the valley gives you a chance to explore them. There are castles at Aspe, Novelda (➤ 43), Monforte del Cid (Monforte del Sit), Elda, Petrel (Petrer), and Sax (➤ 48), with Biar (➤ 37) lying a little to the north.

+ 28C4
✉ 60km west of Alicante
🍴 Choice of restaurants and bars (€–€€€)
🚌 From Alicante
🚍 From Alicante
ℹ Villena: Plaza de Santiago 5 ☎ 965 80 38 04
♿ Few
❓ Moros y Cristianos (4–9 Sep)
↔ Biar (➤ 37), Sax (➤ 48)

Museo Arqueológico

✉ Plaza de Santiago 2
☎ (965) 80 11 50 Ext 50
🕐 Tue–Fri 10–2, 5–8, Sat and Sun 11–1:30
♿ Few
💶 Inexpensive

+ 29D3
✉ Starts 30km west of Alicante
🍴 Choice of restaurants everywhere (€–€€)
🚌 From Alicante
ℹ Biar: Avenida de Villena s/n ☎ 965 81 11 77

Left: *outside the Monumento al Coralista – a monument to the Cuban sailors who came to Torrevieja to trade goods.*

Far left: *crowds of bronzed bodies throng the shoreline on sunny summer days at Torrevieja*

Benidorm & the North

The name Benidorm is familiar worldwide, synonymous with packed beaches, high-rise hotels, glitz and fun, a place where millions of visitors let their hair down and enjoy good-value sunshine holidays. Most never stir from the town itself, but for those that do there are huge rewards. Other lively resorts lie on the coast to the north and south, easily reached by the little train which trundles up and down between Alicante (Alacant) and Dénia. Altea, Calpe (Calp), Jávea (Xàbia) and Dénia are all worth visiting for a change of scene and pace, and a chance to discover more traditional resorts. Inland from Benidorm rise some of Spain's most steep and beautiful coastal mountains. This area, dotted with historic towns and villages, planted with almonds, oranges and olives, preserves a way of life untouched by the development of the last 40 years.

' The land also of song and dance, of bright suns and eyes. '

RICHARD FORD
*A Handbook for
Travellers in Spain* (1855)

●

Left: *the graceful curve of the sands at Benidorm, the familiar image of the Costa Blanca*

Benidorm

✚ 29E4

ℹ Avenida Martínez Alejos 16, ☎ 965 85 13 11

❓ Carnaval (Feb), Fallas de San José (16–19 Mar), Semana Santa (Mar/Apr), Festa de la Creu (1 May), Hogueras de San Juan (24 Jun), San Fermín (6–7 Jul), Virgen del Carmen (16 Jul), San Jaime (25 Jul), Moros y Cristianos (end Sep), Fiestas Patronales (mid Nov)

Benidorm, the Mediterranean's largest tourist resort, with over 4 million visitors annually, is a shining example of a superbly organised mass-tourism destination. Love it or hate it, no one can criticise the slickness and efficiency of the operation, which truly provides 'something for everyone'. Winter and summer alike, Benidorm has got the formula right for visitors of every age.

Benidorm was first settled by the Moors, and developed as a tiny fishing village whose castle was constantly attacked by pirates from North Africa and the Berber coast.

Above: *all visitors find their way through Benidorm's old quarter to the Mirador lookout*

Opposite: *Aigüera Park is at its most peaceful in the early morning*

By the 1600s this threat had diminished, the parish church was built, and the fishermen were acquiring an international reputation as tuna fishers. The town became one of many similar coastal settlements, and it was not until the late 19th century that the attractions of its micro-climate began to be known. The first tourists were Spanish, who came in increasing, but still minimal, numbers up to the 1950s. More leisure and higher incomes coincided with cheaper air travel, and throughout the 1960s Benidorm's growth was spectacular. Hotels, apartment buildings, shops, restaurants and recreational facilities proliferated, the Spanish learned what foreign holiday-makers expected, and Benidorm's economic future was assured. Today, Benidorm will either provide everything you need on holiday, or make a good base from which to explore the more traditional Spain only a few kilometres inland.

What to See in Benidorm

CASTILLO-MIRADOR ✪
Nothing remains of Benidorm's castle, thought to have been built before the town's first charter was issued in 1325. It was strategically sited at the highest point of the original settlement on the promontory now occupied by the old village. Its story was one of repeated attacks by Algerian and Berber pirates. Plaintive documents exist imploring the king for money to repair it throughout the 16th century. It was finally blown up in 1812 and its ruins had disappeared by the beginning of the 20th century. Its old site, now a charming square by a church, is a favourite look-out point with sweeping views of Benidorm's superb beaches.

✚ 29E4
✉ Plaza de Castillo
🍴 Several bars on the square
♿ Few

IGLESIA DE SAN JAIME ✪
St James is the parish church of Benidorm, beautifully sited on the old town's promontory overlooking the sea. Building started in 1740, the same year as the discovery of the statue of Our Lady of the Sorrows, the town's patron saint. At this date Benidorm was expanding considerably on tuna-fishing profits, which helped fund the church's construction. With its blue-tiled domes and white walls, it is typical of all traditional churches along the coast, and for local people is still very much the heart of the town.

✚ 29E4
✉ Plaza Castelar
♿ Good
 Free

LA ISLA DE BENIDORM ✪
A mere 20-minute boat trip across the bay, Benidorm Island makes a good destination for a picnic and swim. Rising at one end to sheer cliffs, its clear deep waters are ideal for snorkelling and scuba diving. The island is uninhabited except for gulls and other seabirds, and is a designated sanctuary. You can get there in an 'aquascope' boat, whose transparent hull lets you see underwater.

✚ 29E4
🍴 Summer-only bar
🚢 Barco a la Isla, Puerto de Benidorm
☎ 965 85 00 52

PARQUE DE L'AIGÜERA ✪
Benidorm is justly proud of Aigüera Park, a long sweep of promenades, fountains and greenery running seawards down a dried-up river valley. It was designed by the post-Modernist Catalan architect Ricardo Bofill. It was the first major piece of public architecture in Benidorm, designed to add some sophistication to a resort that was tired of being branded 'down-market'. It succeeded brilliantly, its elegant central avenue acting as a meeting place and its two fine amphitheatres, dramatically lit at night, are ideal for concerts and cultural events.

✚ 29E4
✉ Avenida de l'Aigüera
🍴 Bars (€)
♿ Excellent Free

♔ 29E4
✉ Avenida d'Alcoi/Avenida de Madrid
🍴 Huge choice of restaurants and bars near by
♿ Good

PLAYA DE LEVANTE ●●

Backed by towering hotels, the 2km-long curve of golden sand known as the Playa de Levante swarms with crowds day and night. For most visitors the beach epitomises Benidorm's attractions – hot sun, clear blue water, clean white sand. Packed in summer, it offers wonderful chances to make friends from all over the world, to show off, and to indulge in some serious people-watching yourself. At night it's transformed into a brilliantly sparkling chain of lights, the perfect backdrop for the resort's vibrant night scene.

♔ 29E4
✉ Avenida de la Armada Española
🍴 Huge choice of restaurants and bars near by
♿ Good

PLAYA DE PONIENTE ●

Poniente is Benidorm's other beach, just as long, clean and beautiful as Levante and situated on the other side of the old town. Not quite as central, it is ideal for families with young children and older people. Like Levante, its promenade is thronged for the evening *paseo* and glitters with myriad lights at night.

Right: *as night falls on Benidorm, waterfront lights twinkle along its corniche*

Below: *early sunbathers catching the morning rays at Playa de Levante*

Did you know ?

Despite an average of 45,000 people using them every day in summer, Benidorm's beaches and waters are among the world's cleanest. Rubbish is collected at dusk and machines sift and oxygenate the sand during the night. The seawater is constantly cleaned and monitored by a filtration plant in the bay.

Around Benidorm

Start at the seafront at the corner of Avenida d'Alcoi and Avenida Martínez Alejos and walk inland for 100m. Turn left into old Benidorm, a fishing village until the 1960s, along Gats Ricardo, and go up the steps of the delightful Carrer dels Gats to Plaça del Castell.

This pretty clifftop square, dominated by the blue-domed church of San Jaime (➤ 57), gives wonderful views of the whole stretch of Benidorm Bay, with Playa de Levante (➤ 58) to the north and Playa de Poniente (➤ 58) to the south. The dramatic promontory beyond Poniente is the Sierra Helada (Serra Gelada, ➤ 74).

Turn south to the Plaça de la Senyoria, take the flight of steps, left, down to the jetty, turn right along Passeig de Colon and right again along Passeig de la Carretera, the old town's main street.

The blue-tiled dome of San Jaime is typical of churches in Costa Blanca

Look out on your left for the entrance to the covered Mercado Municipal, packed with fascinating fish and meat stalls and a good place to buy a picnic. Turn left on to Calle Tomás Ortuño (not marked on the turning), narrow here, but widening as it runs uphill towards the new part of town, and full of general food and household shops.

Take a right turn down Calle Escoles, and cross the junction to Calle Hondo. A short flight of steps leads down to the Parque de L'Aigüera (➤ 57), a haven of green and soothing fountains. Walk up through the park to the top left-hand gate; from here Benidorm's impressive Plaza de Toros can be seen above. Cross the Avenida de L'Aigüera and go through Calle San Marco to rejoin Tomás Ortuño.

Distance
2.5km

Time
1½–2 hours

Start point
Avenida d'Alco
🚌 3, 12

End point
West end of Calle Tomás Ortuña
🚌 6

Lunch
Pulpo Pirata (€)
✉ Calle Tomás Ortuña
☎ 966 80 32 19

59

Right: *white houses with ornate ironwork* rejas *line Altea's narrow streets*
Inset: *the lovely blue domes of La Virgen de la Consuelo, Altea*

+ 29E4
⊠ 12km north of Benidorm
❚❙ Restaurants/bars (€–€€€)
🚌 From Benidorm
🚌 From Benidorm
ℹ Carrer Sant Pere 9
   ☎ 965 84 41 22 / 965 84 41 14
❓ Fogueras de Sant Joan (24 Jun), San Pedro (Jul/Aug), Moros y Cristianos (last week of Sep)
↔ Benidorm (► 55–9), Calpe (► 62)

+ 29F4
⊠ 26km north of Benidorm
❚❙ Restaurants/bars (€–€€)
🚌 From Benidorm
🚌 From Benidorm
ℹ Avenida País Valencià 1
   ☎ 965 73 22 25
❓ Fira i Porrat di Sant Antoni (3 weeks in Jan)

What to See in the North

ALTEA ✪✪

Sheltered and encircled by steep hills and cliffs, Altea tumbles down the slopes below the blue-tiled domed church of La Virgen de la Consuelo, sitting at the highest point of the picturesque old village like a cherry on a cake. A Roman settlement, the original fishing village was restored by a colony of artists in the 1950s and a variety of painters, craftsmen and potters are still among its inhabitants. Their sense of style spills over into the steep white streets, shaded by orange trees, festooned with geraniums and lined with tempting boutiques. Inevitably such charms, and Altea's proximity to Benidorm, attract huge numbers of visitors. The beach is backed by a pleasant palm-lined esplanade with a wide range of restaurants, and there are good watersports facilities.

BENISSA ✪

Deliberately built inland from the coast to escape the Berber raids, the streets of the historic old town of Benissa slope gently downhill. This tawny-coloured town, with its one long main street shaded with orange trees, seems a million miles from the razzmatazz of the big coastal resorts. Lovely old houses and mansions, the gable and porch designs clearly Moorish, and the windows protected by the traditional *rejas*, line streets such as the Calle de la Purísima. The huge church of the Purísima, known as La Catedral de la Marina, dominates the central square, planted with palms and cooled by fountains. At the top of the town stands the peaceful Franciscan Convento de la Purísima, and there's an odd little Museo Etnológico (ethnographic museum) in the 15th-century agricultural exchange.

CABO DE LA NAO (CAP DE LA NAU)

The headland of Cabo de la Nao, the most easterly point on the Costa Blanca, soars above the sea to the south of Jávea (Xàbia). This stretch of coast makes a wonderful contrast to the flat sandy beaches to the north. Creamy white and ochre-tinted cliffs rise steeply from the sea below, the slopes clad in pines and sweet-smelling scrub vegetation. Unsurprisingly, the tourist boom attracted developers, and much of the surrounding area is dotted with secluded holiday villas. From the cape and its lighthouse there are superb views along the cliffs to the south and a road leads on to the lovely cove at Granadella (➤ 83). South of here there are no roads and experienced walkers can enjoy the unspoiled coast.

- 🔢 29F5
- ✉ 50km north of Benidorm
- 🍴 Restaurant and bars (€–€€)
- ♿ Few
- ↔ Cabo de San Martín (➤ 61), Jávea (➤ 71), Moraira (➤ 72)

CABO DE SAN MARTÍN (CAP DE SANT MARTÍ) ⭐

The beautiful bay of Jávea is sheltered at its southern end by the Cabo de San Martín, a rocky promontory where it is easy to escape the crowds of the nearby beaches. South of Jávea (➤ 71) a path drops from the road at the Cruz de Portichol, a stone wayside cross from where both the cape and the island of Portichol (Isla de Portitxol) are visible. This leads out to San Martín, running through clumps of lavender, thyme and rosemary, to emerge at the headland. The all-round views are excellent; north to the town and beaches of Jávea, south to precipitous cliffs and the island. Other tracks lead up and down the coast, one to Cala Sardinera (➤ 82), a secluded little beach.

- 🔢 29F5
- ✉ 50km north of Benidorm
- ♿ None
- ↔ Cabo de la Nao (➤ 61), Jávea (➤ 71), Dénia (➤ 63)

Portichol lies just off the headland of Cabo de San Martín

CALPE (CALP)

The coast north of Benidorm has a chain of good beaches, classy villas hidden behind bougainvillaea-hung walls and relaxed family resorts. Calpe is one of the most popular of these, due mainly to the soaring mass of the Peñón de Ifach (➤ 23). This former fishing village, with its *mudéjar* church, towers, walls and museums (Museo Arqueológico and Museo Fester), was particularly stalwart during the years of Berber pirate invasion; so much so that Carlos V dubbed it '*muy heroica villa*'. Its two splendid sandy beaches are often crowded in summer, but you can escape to sea for a boat trip round the Peñón or take a stroll near the salt flats behind town. Calpe is a good place to get the feel of this coast, with well-stocked cheerful shops and outdoor restaurants. It has a lively nightlife during the summer, and is known for its sporting facilities.

COCENTAINA ⭐⭐

The thriving inland town of Cocentaina in the Serpis valley is one of the most historic in the area, its medieval Christian and Arab quarters still clearly delineated below its ancient castle. Packed with fine old buildings and churches, the town is noted for its fiestas and superb local cooking. The major tourist attraction is the Palau Comtal, a magnificent, and recently restored, 13th–15th century fortified palace. Its lovely rooms include the Sala Dorada and the Sala de Embajadores, with tiled Renaissance floors and exuberant baroque ceilings. The most notable church is the Mare Déu, and there are two museums, the Museu del Centre d'Estudis Contestans, featuring the whole story of Cocentaina with displays and an audio-visual programme, and the Casa Museu del Fester, devoted to the Moros y Cristianos festival.

COLL DE RATES ⭐⭐

The Coll de Rates road (➤ 73), less than 20 minutes' drive from Benidorm, is one of the most scenic on the Costa Blanca and gives a chance for a quick and easy taste of the beauty of the inland sierras. The road climbs and twists steadily through mountain scenery to the pass, which lies at 780m. From the north the rise is gradual, the fertile agricultural plain dropping away and the vegetation changing as views of the sea emerge. Through the coll, the southern landscape is enclosed by the dramatic Parcent and Aixorta mountains.

DÉNIA ⬤⬤

Lying beneath the heights of the Montgó natural park, (➤ 22) historic and elegant Dénia is a far less brash holiday resort than some of its neighbours. Inhabited by the Phoenicians and the Greeks, it was named in honour of the Roman goddess Diana; the inhabitants are still known as *dianenses*. English raisin-dealers lived here throughout the 19th century and many are buried in the almost-forgotten English cemetery; the town's broad streets and solid buildings date from this time. A small Museo Etnológico has displays on the town's early history. Dénia's other attractions include the Castillo de Dénia (castle), perched high above the town and housing a small Museo Arqueológico (archaeological museum), the lovely 18th-century Church of the Assumption, and a picturesque old quarter near the fishing port. From here, ferries run to the Balearic Islands and a narrow-gauge train runs down the coast to Alicante (Alacant). But a car is probably the best way to see the lovely coastline to the south (➤ 82).

Left: *the beachside promenade at Calpe is popular with strollers*

🏠 29F5
✉ 55km north of Benidorm
🍴 Choice of restaurants and bars (€–€€€)
🚌 From Benidorm
⛴ To Ibiza and Palma, Mallorca: Flebasa Lines, Estación Marítima
☎ 965 78 76 06, daily 9PM
ℹ Oculista Buigues 9
☎ 966 42 23 67
❓ Fallas de San José (16–19 Mar), Romería a la Virgen de Rocio (Jun), Hogueras de San Juan (20–24 Jun), Fiesta de la Santísima Sangre (2nd Wed after 28 Jun), Moros y Cristianos y San Roque (14–16 Aug)
↔ Jávea (➤ 71)

Did you know ?

In the middle of the 19th century more than 75 per cent of the raisins imported into the United States and Britain came from Dénia. Grown on specially trained vines, the grapes were picked and dried by a mixture of sunshine and artificial heat.

Below: *the brightly painted buildings of Dénia's old quarter*

The Coast from Dénia to Benissa

Distance
65km

Time
About 2½ hours or all day with stops for sightseeing and swimming

Start point
Dénia
✚ 29F5

End point
Benissa
✚ 29F4

Lunch
Bar-Restaurante Cabo La Nao
(€€)
✉ Faro Cabo La Nao
☎ 965 77 18 35

Benissa's narrow white streets look their best when decorated for a local festival

Did you know ?

There are nearly a hundred castles in the Costa Blanca area, most originally built by the Moors between the 8th and 13th centuries. They were all designed for protection against outside threats, which ranged from tax collectors and neighbouring feudal lords to foreign invaders and pirates.

Take the AP132 east from Dénia through the fringes of the Montgó natural park (➤ 22). After 6.5km turn left on to Carretera el Cap de Sant Antoni.

This road runs through an unspoiled tract of pines and scrub to the Cabo de San Antonio (➤ 22), with its lighthouse and superb views.

Backtrack to the main road and turn left to visit Jávea (Xàbia, ➤ 71). Head south past the beaches and take the A1334 to Cabo de la Nao (➤ 61), branching left on to the AP1331, which runs out to the point.

The road runs through pine woods dotted with enviable villas and side-tracks leading down to hidden beaches. It's worth making the detour to Playa de la Barraca (➤ 83) before continuing to the cape, with another lighthouse and a wonderful cliff vista.

Retrace your route up from the beach and after 2km turn left on to the AV1332 to La Granadella (➤ 83), another sheltered cove. Drive almost back to Jávea then turn left and left again, following signs to Benitatxell on an unclassified road running through vineyards. At the T-junction turn left on to the AV1341 to Benitatxell itself, a laid-back village. Continue on the AV1341 through Teulada and turn right on the N332 (which is signposted C332) to Benissa (➤ 60).

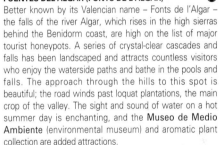

A cooling glimpse of the main falls at Algar

FUENTES DEL ALGAR (FONTS DE L'ALGAR)

Better known by its Valencian name – Fonts de l'Algar – the falls of the river Algar, which rises in the high sierras behind the Benidorm coast, are high on the list of major tourist honeypots. A series of crystal-clear cascades and falls has been landscaped and attracts countless visitors who enjoy the waterside paths and bathe in the pools and falls. The approach through the hills to this spot is beautiful; the road winds past loquat plantations, the main crop of the valley. The sight and sound of water on a hot summer day is enchanting, and the **Museo de Medio Ambiente** (environmental museum) and aromatic plant collection are added attractions.

29E4
16km from Benidorm
Bars and restaurants near by (€–€€)
Guadalest (► 20), Polop (► 72)

Museo de Medio Ambiente
965 88 21 06
10–7
Few
Moderate

GANDÍA

It is hardly surprising that Gandía, with over 20km of clean golden sand, an elegant promenade and animated restaurants, promotes itself as a beach resort (► 83). Tourism began here in the 1950s and many visitors never go near Gandía proper, a largely modern city on the river Serpis. It flourished in the 15th century, its wealth derived from sugar and silk, its political clout from its Borja dukes. The main monuments date from this time, grouped close together near the river in the oldest part of town. The star attraction is the Palacio de Santo Duque, a sumptuous 14th- to 17th-century pile built round a courtyard, its interior dripping with gold leaf; look out for the beautiful *azulejos* and Arab wall tiles. The collegiate church of Santa María is an austere and serene example of Catalan Gothic and the old medieval hospital now houses the town's Museo Arqueológico (archaeological museum). Gandía prides itself on its markets and shops.

29E5
70km north of Benidorm
Choice of restaurants and bars (€–€€€)
From Benidorm
Marqués de Campo s/n 962 87 77 88; Paseo Neptuno s/n 962 87 77 88/ 962 84 24 07
Fallas de San José (16–19 Mar), Semana Santa (Mar/Apr), Hogueras de San Juan (24 Jun), Virgen del Carmen (16 Jul), San Francisco de Borja (29 Sep–3 Oct)
Oliva (► 72)

*Almond terraces below
the fortress of Guadalest,
with the high sierras
rising behind*

GORGOS VALLEY ✪

The river Gorgos is joined by the river Castell west of the little town of Gata de Gorgos, and runs into the sea at Jávea (Xàbia, ➤ 71). The landscape of this gentle agricultural valley, surrounded by gradually rising hills, is known for its citrus groves and its vineyards. Here the traditional way of life has been untouched by the coastal tourist boom. Gata itself straddles the main road, but the peaceful old town makes a good stop, especially if you're interested in cane and rattan ware. Cane and esparto grass have been used here for centuries to make the matting and furniture still on sale today, though much is now imported. West from Gata, orange groves start to give way to vineyards. The traditional grape here is the *moscatello*, used in the production of wines of the same name, still a speciality of Alicante (Alacant) province. The raisins made from these grapes were famed in the 19th century, when they were shipped from Dénia (➤ 63). The attractive old houses, now largely uninhabited, are called *ríu-raus*; their arched porches were designed for drying the grapes. Jalón (Xaló) lies surrounded by this fertile land, a tranquil town with a striking church and local wine for sale in its shops. From here the valley narrows, the sierras rise on either side, and the villages become more scattered.

GUADALEST VALLEY ✪✪✪

Most visitors to the Costa Blanca make the trip to the castle at Guadalest (➤ 20), but few explore further into the valley, one of the most beautiful in the province. Blessed by the Guadalest river and abundant springs, it was first terraced and irrigated by the Moors, and is sheltered on all sides by high mountains and dramatic peaks. These create a micro-climate ideal for the wide range of fruit trees that have been grown here for centuries. The oranges and loquats of the lower slopes give way to almonds as the road climbs; in early spring the entire hillside is a sea of pink blossom. Olive trees gradually appear to replace the almonds, only to give way to pine and mountain shrubs as the road reaches its highest point at the Puerto de Ares, from where another valley system opens out towards Alcoy (Alcoi, ➤ 36). Among the white villages strung along the valley road (➤ 49) are Benifato, Benimantell, Beniardá and Confrides. Stop in these villages to wander the quaint streets, hung with bougainvillaea and geraniums, and absorb the grandeur of the encircling mountains.

Játiva (Xàtiva)

The ancient settlement of Játiva lies less than an hour from the coast. Here the Iberians prospered and minted coinage, only to be ousted first by the Romans and then by Hannibal's Carthaginians on their way to Rome. A Visigothic episcopal seat, the town was conquered by the Moors in the 10th century, and it was from Játiva that they introduced paper manufacture to Europe. Jaime I took the town in 1244 and its fortunes waxed and waned over the following centuries. Burnt in 1707, it was rebuilt but gradually lost its political importance. The birthplace of two Borgia popes (born 'Borja' in Spain) and the painter El Españoleto, Játiva today offers a perfect contrast to the modern coastal resorts.

➕ 29D5
✉ 110km nothwest of Benidorm
🍴 Choice of restaurants and bars (€–€€€)
🚌 From Alicante
ℹ Alameda de Jaume I, 50
   ☎ 962 27 33 46

The best way to get a feel of the town is to walk, following the route marked on the useful leaflet you can pick up at the tourist office. The old quarter, its streets lined with stately mansions, runs along the side of the hill that overlooks the whole town. A road runs up this hill to the magnificent castle (► 68), occupying virtually the entire ridge, and goes past the lovely early church of San Feliu (Sant Feliu, ► 24). It's a tough walk, so the twice-daily tourist train might prove useful. The panoramic views from the top help explain Játiva's historical and strategic importance through the centuries. Back down the hill a broad avenue of plane trees divides the old centre from the modern town.

The castle ramparts of Játiva give superb views of the town and surrounding farmland

What to See in Játiva

✉ Carretera Castillo
🕐 Oct–Apr, Tue–Sun 10–6;
May–Sep, Tue–Sun 10–7
🍴 Bar within castle walls (€)
🚌 Tourist train from outside
tourist office Mon–Sat
12:30, 4:30; Sun 12, 1,
4:30
♿ None
✊ Moderate
❓ Occasional summer
concerts – ask at tourist
office

EL CASTELL   ●●

This huge fortress, stretching along a ridge, dominates the town. Actually two castles, one pre-Roman and one later, its towered walls are still impressive and it's easy to see why it was considered one of the most secure in the region. The section known as the lower castle is the older, the majority of its surviving walls and towers built by the Moors. It occupies the site of the Iberian, Roman and Carthaginian fortress and some sections of the stonework date from Roman times. The Queen's Tower is said to be named after Hannibal's wife, who gave birth to a son here. The upper castle is much larger; a confusing succession of ancient gateways, crumbling courtyards, guardrooms, and towers. Highlights are the tiny and beautiful Gothic chapel of Santa María, reconstructed in 1431 on an earlier site, and a series of Arabic cisterns and watchtowers. The view from the highest point is well worth the climb; the town lies directly below, with ranges of hills to the south and the ancient frontier with Castile to the east.

✉ Corretgeria 46
☎ 962 27 65 97
🕐 Mid-Sep to mid-Jun, Tue–
Fri 10–2, 4–6, Sat and
Sun 10–2; mid-Jun to
mid-Sep, Tue–Sun 10–2
♿ Good
✊ Moderate

MUSEO MUNICIPAL DE ALMUDÍ   ●

Housed in the mid-16th-century municipal granary, Játiva's town museum is worth a visit for the building alone. The Gothic façade hides a spacious Renaissance interior built around a graceful columned courtyard, all imaginatively restored as a backdrop for the collections. The archaeological treasures include Iberian and Roman artefacts and some fine Moorish ceramics and fragments of buildings. The picture collection has paintings by José Ribera, later known as El Españoleto, born here in 1591, and a loan collection of mainly 17th-century works from the Prado in Madrid. Look for the Goya engravings and the portrait of Philip V, hung permanently upside down in retribution for his burning of Játiva during the War of the Spanish Succession.

THE OLD TOWN ⊙⊙

As you wander the peaceful streets of the old town, there are some wonderful churches and buildings to admire, many dating from Játiva's rebuilding after Philip V burnt the town in 1707. Among them is the collegiate church of La Seu, built with Borja money in 1596, a vast Renaissance structure with a Gothic nave. Opposite stands the Hospital Real, dating from the 15th century, its lovely façade adorned with a ring of beautifully carved angels encircling the Madonna over the main door. Look out, too, for the Romanesque church of San Francisco, Sant Pere and the house where Borja Pope Alexander II was born. Other fine mansions include the Palacio del Marqués de Montortal, a lovely 15th-century building with later additions, and the 19th-century Casa de Diego. The old town's streets are punctuated with little plazas, many of them filled with the sound of splashing water from the numerous fountains. The simple one in the tiny plaza outside the Palace of Justice is Gothic in style and the town's only surviving medieval fountain. On the edge of the old quarter you'll find the Font de las 25 Canelles, a fountain erected in 1794 with 25 spouts. Surprises are around every corner – peaceful squares and graceful mansions, with the added attraction that few tourists have yet discovered Játiva.

SAN FELIU (SANT FELIU, ➤ 24, TOP TEN)

Left: *it's well worth the steep climb to visit the castle at Játiva*
Below: *the Virgin and Child graces the Hospital Real's main door, Játiva*
Bottom: *the harmonious façade of the hospital*

JÁVEA (XÀBIA) ✪✪

Jávea, today known mainly as a friendly family resort, had a long and respectable history before its spread down the hill towards the beautiful and protected beaches. Believed to be the sunniest place on the coast, the town lies on a bay embraced by the promontories of Cabo de San Antonio (Cap de Sant Antoni, ➤ 22) to the north and pine-studded Cabo de la Nao (Cap de la Nau, ➤ 61) to the south. The narrow streets of the old town are lined with handsome houses, ornamented with delicate stonework and wrought-iron *rejas* and balconies. Fine buildings cluster around the Plaza de la Iglesia, with its fortified Gothic church of San Bartolomé and dignified town hall.

Just down the street the local Museo Arqueológico, Histórico y Etnográfico (archaeological, historical and ethnographic museum) is housed in a Gothic palace; it traces Jávea's history from Iberian and Roman times to the emergence of the Christian kingdoms, and gives pride of place to replicas of exquisite Iberian gold jewellery found near by. The port area, called the Aduanas de Mar, has a busy working harbour. Here you'll find the fish market and fishing boats, the modern church of Nuestra Señora de Loreto with its roof like a ship's hull, long stretches of safe beach and shops, bars and restaurants. Jávea, with its good facilities, friendly atmosphere, and easy access to the unspoiled country of Montgó (➤ 22) is a popular base for holiday-makers of all ages.

Balanced architectural detail enhances many of the houses in Jávea's old centre

➕ 29F5
✉ 55km north of Benidorm
🍴 Choice of restaurants and bars (€–€€€)
🚍 From Benidorm
ℹ Jávea: Plaza Almirante Bastarreche 11, Aduanas de Mar ☎ 965 79 07 36; Plaza de la Iglesia 4 ☎ 965 79 43 56
❓ Fogueras de Sant Joan (24 Jun), Moros y Cristianos (last weekend in Jul), Nuestra Señora de Loreto (1–8 Sep)
↔ Dénia (➤ 63), Montgó (➤ 22)

MORAIRA ✪

As much an area as a village, Moraira's name for many people is synonymous with expensive second homes and resident expatriates. Originally a fishing village on a sheltered bay below a rocky headland, Moraira lies well off the main coast road and is undisturbed by the sort of crowds that flock to the main resorts. Many spacious villas are scattered among the pine woods that run down to the sea, but with only a handful of hotels, Moraira remains one of the most unspoiled resorts, with a variety of services aimed specifically at its foreign residents. A lovely coastline, a superbly restored 18th-century castle, good sports facilities, upmarket shops and one of Spain's best restaurants, Girasol (➤ 97), all tempt visitors to return.

➕ 29F4
✉ 35km from Benidorm
🍴 Choice of restaurants and bars (€–€€€)
ℹ Carretera Moraira-Teulada 51 ☎ 965 74 51 68
♿ Few
↔ Benissa (➤ 60), Calpe (➤ 62)

Opposite: statue of Játiva-born painter José de Ribera (1591–1652)

⊞ 29E5
✉ 42km north of Benidorm
🍴 Choice of restaurants and bars (€–€€€)
ℹ Passeig Lluís Vivès s/n
   ☎ 962 85 55 28
↔ Gandía (➤ 65)

Children of all ages enjoy Oliva's sandy beaches

⊞ 29E4
✉ 12km north of Benidorm
🍴 Choice of restaurants and bars (€–€€€)
🚌 From Benidorm
ℹ Polop de la Marina: Carretera Benidorm, Polop Esq G Miró-Teuleria
   ☎ 966 89 60 72
? San Roque (15 Aug), San Francisco de Borja (4 Oct)
↔ Guadalest (➤ 20), Guadalest valley (➤ 66), Benidorm (➤ 55–9)

OLIVA ✪

North of Jávea (Xàbia) the coastline is flatter, becoming an almost continuous strip of smooth sandy beaches, ideal for small children and their families. The coastal towns and resorts cater efficiently for large numbers of summer visitors, with hotels, restaurants, sports facilities, marinas, entertainment and shops. Playa de Oliva is one of these, but inland lies the old town, once part of a dukedom founded in 1449 by Alfonso el Magnánimo, with the remnants of the old ducal castle to be found outside the town. The surrounding flat, fertile ground, now planted with oranges, was originally marshland, and some wetlands remain. The old town centre has some fine 16th-century buildings and the wonderfully higgledy-piggledy white-washed quarter of Santa Ana.

POLOP ✪

Few visitors bother to stop at Polop, a foothill town on the Guadalest road, but this small white-washed *pueblo* is well worth the easy trip from Benidorm. A visit here is a chance to see an everyday inland town, largely untouched by the development seen on the coast. Lovely old buildings line the narrow streets, the church is a fine example of local architecture, and a ruined castle and a clutch of good restaurants complete the picture. The main attraction is the Font Els Xorros, an ancient fountain with 221 spouts which has been renovated, but the Museo del Alambre, with its medieval basement, is also worth a quick visit. Polop has always been noted for its craftwork, and lace, embroidery and woollen goods in traditional styles and patterns are still made locally.

From Pego to La Nucia

Start at Pego and leave the town by the C3318 (715) heading southeast to the hills of the Sierra de Alfaro and the Sierra de Aixorta.

Once surrounded by rice fields, the lively town of Pego feels a long way from the coastal resorts. It still retains its wide town gates and the parish church has a lovely 15th-century altarpiece of the pregnant Madonna.

The route follows the C3318 (715) to Orba. Leave the town and follow the road into the hills towards the Coll de Rates pass (➤ 62).

As the road climbs superb views open out towards the coast: villages scattered across the plain, a patchwork of fields and ever-widening glimpses of the sea and the coastal massifs. There are several points where you can admire the views.

Once over the pass continue on the C3318 (715) all the way to Polop (➤ 72) and La Nucia.

Over the pass the scenery becomes, if possible, more breathtaking as the road descends towards the Guadalest valley and the Fuentes del Algar (Fonts de l'Algar, ➤ 65). Terraces are planted with almonds, loquats and oranges and the dramatic crags of Aixorta rise up to the south. La Nucia is worth a stop, particularly on a Sunday when it hosts a large street market.

Visit Pego and its old church before exploring the surrounding countryside

Distance
55km

Time
2 hours without stops, all day with visits and shopping

Start point
Pego
✚ 29E5

End point
La Nucia
✚ 29E4

Lunch
Ca L'Angeles (€€)
✉ Gabriel Miró 16, Polop
☎ (965) 87 02 26

➕ 29E4
✉ 30km west of Benidorm
🍴 Restaurants and bars
(€–€€€)
↔ Guadalest valley (➤ 66)

*The dramatic mountains
of the Sierra de Aitana
rise up behind the
Benidorm coast*

➕ 29E4
✉ 2km north of Benidorm
🍴 None
🚌 From Benidorm
ℹ Benidorm: Avenida
Martinez Alejos 16
☎ 966 80 59 14
♿ None
↔ Benidorm (➤ 55–9)

SIERRA DE AITANA (SERRA D'AITANA)

When the coast is sweltering in the summer heat, it's tempting to head for the hills. Easily accessible from Alicante (Alacant) and Benidorm, the Sierra de Aitana makes a good choice, with attractions for all the family, breathtaking mountain scenery, fresh breezes and cooler temperatures. The range takes its name from the peak of Aitana, at 1,558m the highest summit in the Costa Blanca's northern sierras. You can drive nearly to the top and there are wonderful views over woodland to the surrounding mountains and the coast. Excellent hiking country, the Sierra has good trails and paths and picnic areas for families; children will enjoy the area's safari park (➤ 111). On the edge of the mountains, the pretty villages of Sella and Alcolecha (Alcoleja) are worth a visit; both have good restaurants.

SIERRA HELADA (SERRA GELADA)

Benidorm is sheltered to the north by the Sierra Helada, the ice hills, a mountainous promontory so-called for its lower temperatures and the optical effect of moonlight on its rocky slopes. Riddled with caves used by the Iberians, the headland was mined by the Phoenicians and Romans, and two watchtowers bear witness to its role as a look-out point during the 17th-century pirate raids. The 21st century has left the Sierra untouched, and within a ten-minute bus ride from downtown Benidorm you can find a variety of beautiful hill walks. Tracks lead out to the headlands of Punta de la Escaleta and the lighthouse at Punta Bombarda, while a magnificent path runs along the crest of the ridge, overlooking the sea and coastline.

VILLAJOYOSA (LA VILA JOIOSA) ✪

Ancient Villajoyosa, 'the jewelled town', with its Roman and Moorish origins, started modern life as a fishing village, protected by encircling walls and huddled round its massive and beautiful Gothic church. The old quarter, with its brightly coloured houses in blue and green and ochre, is still the heart of what has become a popular holiday town, with a long sandy beach and everything for the modern visitor, including the **Museo Etnográfico** (ethnographic museum) and the Costa Blanca's main casino. Villajoyosa is at its most exuberant in July, when the week-long Moros y Cristianos festival takes place, one of the region's most rumbustious. Splendidly costumed as Moors, Christians, pirates and slave-girls, locals re-enact key events, including the sacking of the town's castle by the dastardly pirate Zala Arráez in 1538.

Did you know ?

Many of Spain's historic and colourful traditional festivals are considered of such cultural interest that they are designated by the government as being of national tourist interest, for Spaniards as well as foreigners. On the Costa Blanca, Elche, Alcoy, Villajoyosa and Alicante all have such events.

+ 29E4
- 10km south of Benidorm
- Choice of restaurants and bars (€–€€€)
- From Benidorm
- From Benidorm
- Costera del Mar s/n
  ☎ 966 85 13 71
- Virgen del Carmen (15–16 Jul), Moros y Cristianos (24–31 Jul)
- Benidorm (➤ 55–9), Cuevas de Canalobre (➤ 37)

Museo Etnográfico
- Barranquet 1
- ☎ 965 89 16 98
- Mon–Fri 10–1:30, 5–7, Sat 10–1:30
- Few
- Inexpensive

These brightly painted houses typify the colourful architecture of Villajoyosa

Murcia

The province of Murcia lies south of Alicante (Alacant) and stretches inland to Albacete and southwards to Almería. Known since Moorish times for the fertility of its land, Murcia's agriculture has prospered as its once-rich mines have declined. Much of the province is planted with fruit, olives, rice, nuts and vegetables, particularly around its capital, Murcia. Inland lie arid and beautiful mountain ranges, vineyards, historic towns and forgotten villages, where few tourists venture. The coastline offers a wide variety of scenery, from the shallow waters and flat landscapes of the Mar Menor to the secret coves and empty beaches around Mazarrón. This area is popular with holidaying Spaniards, particularly around the Mar Menor, which has the best facilities of Murcia's resorts. From a base here, excursions are possible through undeveloped and little-explored valleys, and superb mountain scenery, to hill towns such as Jumilla and Mula.

> *'…the climate is very mild and favourable… making it possible to enjoy an almost permanent spring.'*
>
> PASCUAL MADOZ
> *An Account of Murcia* (1850)

———————•———————

Left: *flowering plants for sale in Plaza Santo Domingo, old Murcia's largest square*

Spring sunshine tempts Murcian citizens out for a drink on the Glorieta España

✚ 28C2
ℹ Plaza del Romea 4
☎ 902 10 10 70; Plano de San Francisco s/n
☎ 968 35 87 20
❓ Semana Santa (Mar/Apr), Spring Festival (Easter week), Entierra de la Sardina (Easter week)

Museo Arqeológico
✚ 79B3
✉ Gran Via Alfonso X el Sablo 5
☎ 968 23 46 02
🕐 Mon–Fri 9–2, 5–8, Sat 10–2
♿ Good
✋ Moderate

Centro Regional de Artesanía
✉ Francisco Rabal 8
☎ 968 28 45 85
🕐 Mon–Fri 11–2, 4:30–7:30, Sat 11–2, 5–7

Murcia

Founded on the Segura river in the 9th century by the Moors, the city of Murcia soon became an important trading centre, its wealth largely based on the fertility of the outlying *huerta* (market gardens). By the 1300s it was the regional capital and continued to prosper, its 18th-century wealth funding the majority of its finest buildings. Today, it's an agricultural and commercial centre, a delightful and truly Spanish city which makes few concessions to tourism.

It is well worth battling through the modern suburbs to spend time in the historic centre, a largely pedestrianised maze of narrow streets and squares, punctuated by elegant buildings and churches. The major sights, including the magnificent baroque cathedral (➤ 25), cluster around the medieval arteries of the Trapería and Platería, today up-market shopping streets. Here you'll find the bizarre 19th-century Casino (➤ 79), the Teatro Romea, and a clutch of superb churches. Other fine buildings line the river, where there are shady walkways and peaceful green gardens. Murcia is well endowed with museums; the **Museo Arqueológico** (archaeological museum) traces the area's history and the Museo Salzillo (Salzillo Museum ➤ 80) celebrates the wood-carving genius of one of its natives. Local pride in traditional artisan work is evident at the **Centro Regional de Artesanía** (regional crafts centre), and the city has some excellent restaurants specialising in Murcia's vegetable-based cooking.

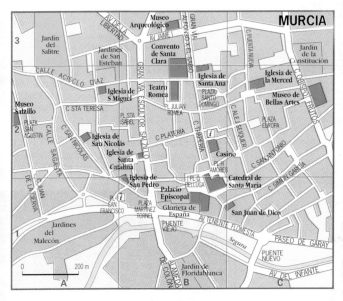

What to See in Murcia

CASINO

⭐⭐

Built between 1847 and 1901, this memorable structure, still in use today, was once the town's main social meeting place, offering members a library, meeting rooms, billiard room and ballroom. An eclectic stylistic mixture of Moorish features, marble and metalwork, French-inspired grandeur, painted ceilings and English craftsmanship, the Casino is high on a must-see list. From the Moorish vestibule a central gallery leads to the library, designed by an English firm and exuding Edwardian rectitude. In stark contrast, the ballroom opposite, with its musicians' gallery, vast painted ceiling and dazzling chandeliers evokes old Vienna, while the high point for most visitors is the ladies' powder room, a neo-baroque fantasy complete with painted ceiling and huge gilt mirrors.

CATEDRAL DE SANTA MARÍA
(► 25, TOP TEN)

A dignified corridor in the Casino leads to the Moorish-style vestibule

🚩 79B2
✉ Calle Traperia 22
☎ 968 21 22 55
🕐 Daily Mon–Sun 10–2, 4:30–8:30
🍴 Bars and restaurants near by (€–€€€)
🎟 Free

⊙ Daily 9–1, 5–7
🎫 Free

CHURCHES ⊙

If you're interested in ecclesiastical architecture, Murcia is full of delights, and fans of the baroque will find many staggering examples of this dramatic and exuberant style. Among the best churches are La Merced, San Miguel, Santa Ana and Santa Clara, grouped together on the edge of the old town, and all with superb façades and Salzillo carvings inside. Another good trio is San Pedro, San Nicolás and Santa Catalina in the same area of town.

✚ 79C2
✉ Obispo Frutos 8
☎ 968 23 93 46
⊙ Mon–Fri 9–2, 5–8, Sat 10–2 (summer 9–1)
♿ Good
🎫 Moderate

MUSEO DE BELLAS ARTES ⊙

A large and variable collection of pictures giving a comprehensive view of the development of Murcian painting from the 15th to the 20th centuries.

Locals relaxing in the narrow Trapería, one of Murcia's prosperous shopping streets

MUSEO DE LA CATEDRAL ⊙

Housed in the cloister of Murcia's great cathedral (➤ 25), this museum houses early sculpture, including a Roman sarcophagus, and gives pride of place to the huge and ornate 600kg gold and silver monstrance, used at the feast of Corpus Christi.

✚ 79C1
✉ Plaza de la Cruz 2
☎ 968 29 18 93
⊙ Oct–Mar daily 10–1, 5–7; Apr–Sep daily 10–1, 5–8
♿ Good 🎫 Inexpensive

MUSEO SALZILLO ⊙

This is probably Murcia's most important museum, displaying a huge collection of work by the 18th-century wood sculptor Francisco Salzillo, born in Murcia. He specialised in dramatic and detailed polychrome figures and scenes from the life of Christ. Most of these were designed to be carried through the streets during the Holy Week processions, as indeed they are still. The nativity scene, with over 500 rustic figures, is worth a close look.

✚ 79A2
✉ Plaza San Agustín 3
☎ 968 29 18 93
⊙ Sep–Jun Tue–Sat 9:30–1, 4–7, Sun 11–1; Jul–Aug, Mon–Fri 9:30–1, 4–7
♿ Few
🎫 Moderate

SAN JUAN DE DIOS ⊙

The oval interior of this flamboyant baroque building has doubled up as both church and museum for some years. The usual Catholic Mass is celebrated every Sunday, but for the rest of the week the church acts as an elegant ecclesiastical backdrop for a fine collection of religious imagery, including works by artists such as Salzillo, Beltrán and Bussy.

✚ 79C1
✉ Eulogio Soriano 4
☎ 968 21 45 41
⊙ Tue–Fri 10–2, 5–8:30, Sat & Sun, 10–2. Closed Aug
♿ Few 🎫 Free

Central Murcia

Start at the Plaza Santo Domingo, the largest open space in Murcia's old quarter with its pavement bars and flower stalls, and head down the Calle Trapería, one of the city centre's smartest shopping streets.

The Casino (➤ 79), with its exotic and opulent interior, is a short way down on the left. The street opens up into the Plaza Hermádez Amores, with the great tower and north façade of the cathedral (➤ 25) in front of you. Cut right down Calle Escultor Salzillo to Plaza Cardinal Belluga, with its fountain and orange trees, where the cathedral's main façade provides a superb contrast to the more sober Renaissance front of the Bishop's Palace to your right.

Walk down the side of the palace, south towards the river and the peaceful terrace of the Glorieta España. From here turn right on the Gran Vía Escultor Salzillo, a busy modern boulevard lined with high-rise buildings and shops. Take the fifth turning to the right and go down Calle Platería, then turn north at the third street on the left to emerge opposite the pale pink 19th-century Teatro Romea. Cut east down any of the narrow alleys leading off the theatre's plaza to arrive back at your starting point in Plaza Santo Domingo.

Distance
1.5km

Time
2–3 hours, depending on visits

Start/end point
Plaza Santo Domingo
✚ 79B2
🚌 3, 4

Lunch
Mesón el Corral de José Luis (€€)
✉ Plaza Santo Domingo 23–24
☎ 968 21 45 97 / 968 21 49 85

Classical lines and muted colours add to the charm of the Teatro Romea

Top Beaches

Far right, top: *some of Costa Blanca's most secluded beaches and coves are often backed by cliffs*

This selection of Costa Blanca's best beaches is listed by town in alphabetical order. 'Facilities' means wheelchair accessibility and the availability of food and drink. Note that some resorts have summer-only bars and restaurants, and few have life-guards on their beaches.

ÁGUILAS (➤ 84)

ALBUFERETA AND SAN JUAN, CABO DE LAS HUERTAS, ALICANTE (ALACANT)

Albufereta has good sandy beaches and small rocky coves. San Juan has 7km of sand shelving in to the sea, hotels, restaurants and sports.

Below: *sandy beaches shelve gently down to clear water.*

PLAYA DEL POSTIGUET, ALICANTE

This Blue Flag beach in the city centre has excellent facilities and clear water, and the marina is an attractive leisure centre.

PLAYA DE PONIENTE AND PLAYA DE LEVANTE, BENIDORM (➤ 58)

CALA SARDINERA, CABO DE SAN MARTÍN (CAP DE SANT MARTÍ) ✚ 29F5

Unspoiled rocky cove with a pebbly beach sheltered by the cliffs on the north side of Cabo San Martín. It's a 15-minute hike through rocks and scrub from the nearest parking, followed by a scramble down – worth every step. No facilities.

CALBLANQUE (➤ 16, TOP TEN)

This nature reserve is fringed by dunes rolling down to sandy beaches. A bumpy track leads to the beach, one of the few untouched stretches on the whole of Spain's Mediterranean coast. Limited facilities.

LES ROTES AND LA MARINETA CASIANA, DÉNIA ✚ 29F5

Two contrasting beaches. If you like swimming off rocks in clear water, Les Rotes fits the bill and good swimmers can follow the cliffs to the south. La Marineta is a long stretch of safe, sandy clean beach backed by a tiled esplanade, excellent for children. Good facilities.

GUARDAMAR DEL SEGURA (➤ 42)

The beach at Guardamar is backed by a unique system of sand dunes, planted with natural pine, eucalyptus and

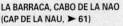

dune-grass, running down to a long beach. Spend the day in the sun or the cool shade of the pines. Good facilities.

LA BARRACA, CABO DE LA NAO (CAP DE LA NAU, ➤ 61)

This is a beautiful curved bay, reached down a twisting road past salubrious villas, and sheltered by high pine-clad cliffs and the island of El Descubridor. Excellent swimming in crystal-clear water off the pebbly beach and plenty of rocks for sunbathing. Reasonable facilities generally available.

LA GRANADELLA, CABO DE LA NAO ✚ 29F5

This justly renowned cove is reached by road through pine woods. There's a sickle-shaped bay, where the pale sands and turquoise sea, scattered with boats, are sheltered by soaring pine-covered cliffs. It can be crowded in summer. Reasonable facilities.

PLAYA DE VENECIA, GANDÍA ✚ 29E5

A huge stretch of immaculately tended white-sand beach with a reputation as one of the liveliest night-time beach areas. Gandía is renowned for its watersports, with sailing and windsurfing top of the list. Excellent facilities.

PLAYA DEL PEDRUCHO, LA MANGA (➤ 86–7)

The long strip of land separating the Mar Menor from the Mediterranean is seldom more than a kilometre across. The warm shallow water beaches on the inner side are ideal for small children, while the windier Mediterranean water shelves more steeply. The facilities are excellent.

Above and below: the perfect bucket and spade holiday for young and old

PLAYA DE OLIVA (➤ 72)

PLAYA DE BOLNUEVO, PUERTO DE MAZARRÓN ✚ 28C1

A large area with a variety of beaches and facilities, Bolnuevo proper has wonderful sand and is sheltered by sandbars; opposite here wind and water have eroded the rocks into fantastic shapes. Hidden coves lie to the south with superb clear water, ideal for snorkelling and scuba diving. Good facilities.

SANTA POLA (➤ 48)

ÁGUILAS ⊗

Well off most foreigners' routes, Águilas is one of the most southerly of the resorts in this area, lying on the Golfo de Mazarrón. This arid stretch of coast is a popular Spanish holiday area that has kept much of its character, and escaped the worst type of development. First inhabited by the Phoenicians, followed by the Romans and Arabs, Águilas's modern appearance dates largely from the 1780s when the present grid-patterned town was built to serve as a port for the local mines. The older fishing quarter, overlooked by the castle of San Juan and the Cope watchtower, still survives; Águilas is still an important port with a daily market. A fine British-built locomotive near the seafront commemorates the importance of the railway in Águilas's economic heyday. Two excellent beaches and a string of virtually undiscovered coves lie on either side of the town, making it a good base if you're looking for a tranquil beach holiday.

➕ 28B1
✉ 80km southeast of Murcia
🍴 Choice of restaurants and bars (€–€€€)
🚃 From Murcia
🚌 From Murcia
ℹ Plaza Antonio Cortijas s/n
☎ 968 48 32 85
↔ Mazarrón (➤ 88)

The crystal waters off Águilas's rocky coast are noted for scuba diving

ALEDO ⊗

The little town of Aledo, situated on the lower slopes of the Sierra de Espuña (➤ 26) and founded as a Moorish stronghold, was once an important frontier town, held from the 13th to the 15th centuries by the Order of Santiago. Today it's a good example of a thriving Murcian country town and a good stopping point if you're driving, its narrow white streets giving glimpses of the fabulous view towards the coast. Just outside is the **Ermita de**

➕ 28B2
✉ 43km south of Murcia
🍴 Choice of restaurants and bars (€–€€)
↔ Totana (➤ 90)

Ermita de Santa Eulalia
🕐 Dawn to dusk

Santa Eulalia, a lovely little building with an exquisite *mudéjar* ceiling and frescoes telling the story of the eponymous saint, hounded to death by Roman soldiers.

CARTAGENA ★

Cartagena, built around a superb natural harbour, was founded by Hannibal as his Iberian capital and named after North African Carthage. A Roman port and administrative centre, its strategic importance continued for centuries, as the numerous surrounding castles and the vast Arsenal testify. Its wealth came from mining, which paid for churches such as Santa Maria de Gracia and La Caridad, as well as the large number of Modernist buildings around the city. Today, the first impression is of a rather run-down industrial city with a naval dockyard and extensive modern suburbs. It's worth persevering, however, as the old city has some of Murcia's best museums, superb architecture, atmospheric streets and old-fashioned shops.

There's a fine view of the harbour and city layout from Parque Torres, from where the road winds back down to the main plaza past the ruined Catedral Vieja, thought to be one of Spain's oldest churches. A palm-lined esplanade runs beside the port to Isaac Perel's submarine, a world-first, built here in 1888. Down in the old town is the church of Santa Maria, with a wonderful collection of carved wooden figures by Salzillo, used in Cartagena's elaborate Holy Week processions. Look out particularly for the Gran Hotel, the Casa Cervantes and Llagostera, all fine Modernist buildings. Museums well worth visiting are the **Museo Arqueológico Municipal**, which traces the city's history and has a large Roman collection, and the **Museo Nacional de Arqueología Marítima**, with many underwater shipwreck finds and a replica of a Roman galley.

+ 28C1

⊠ 53km southeast of Murcia

🍴 Choice of restaurants and bars (€–€€€)

🚌 From Murcia

🚆 From Murcia

ℹ Puertas de San José, Plaza Bastarreche

☎ 968 50 64 83

❓ Carnaval (Feb/Mar), Semana Santa (Mar/Apr), Cartagineses y Romanos (24–30 Sep)

↔ Mar Menor (▶ 86)

Museo Arqueológico Municipal

⊠ Ramón y Cajal 45

☎ 968 12 88 81

🕐 Tue–Fri 10–2, 5–8, Sat and Sun 11–2

♿ Few

💲 Moderate

Museo Nacional de Arqueología Marítima

⊠ Dique de Navidad s/n

☎ 968 12 11 66

🕐 Tue–Sun 10–3

♿ Few

💲 Moderate

Did you know?

The mineral deposits between Cartagena and Murcia were some of the richest in the Mediterranean. Iron, lead, silver, zinc, red ochre and copper were all mined from Carthaginian times.

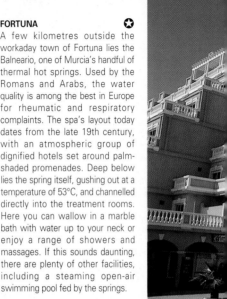

FORTUNA ✪

A few kilometres outside the workaday town of Fortuna lies the Balneario, one of Murcia's handful of thermal hot springs. Used by the Romans and Arabs, the water quality is among the best in Europe for rheumatic and respiratory complaints. The spa's layout today dates from the late 19th century, with an atmospheric group of dignified hotels set around palm-shaded promenades. Deep below lies the spring itself, gushing out at a temperature of 53°C, and channelled directly into the treatment rooms. Here you can wallow in a marble bath with water up to your neck or enjoy a range of showers and massages. If this sounds daunting, there are plenty of other facilities, including a steaming open-air swimming pool fed by the springs.

JUMILLA ✪

Set in the rolling sierras of Murcia's northern corner, Jumilla, a small agricultural and market town well off the beaten track, is a mecca for wine buffs. First planted by the Romans, the vineyards are among Europe's oldest and some of the very few not to have been damaged by the 19th-century phylloxera outbreak. The full-bodied and intense reds have an alcohol content as high as 16 per cent – best drunk mature, the mid-1980s are the years to look out for. You can learn more in the idiosyncratic **Museo del Vino** (wine museum) before a visit to the lovely Franciscan monastery and its little museum, the **Museo Jerónimo Molina**. Other high points here include the castle, a pretty theatre, some fine old mansions around the main square and a remarkable local museum crammed with objects.

MAR MENOR, LA MANGA AND CABO DE PALOS ✪✪

The Mar Menor, Murcia's holiday playground, was formed as sand and rocks gradually advanced outwards from two headlands, slowly transforming the original bay into a vast lagoon. The strip of land separating the lagoon from the Mediterranean is pierced by channels and is called La Manga, 'the sleeve'. This 24km-long ribbon of land, nowhere much more than a kilometre across, was totally undeveloped until the 1960s, a haunt of fishermen and birds. Today it's a solid strip of hotels, apartment blocks, shops, restaurants and bars, catering efficiently for a huge

---

28C3

✉ 22km north of Murcia

🕐 Baths and treatments: daily 7–11:30AM; swimming pool: 10–3

☎ 968 68 50 11

🍴 Restaurant and bar (€–€€)

🚌 From Murcia

🚃 From Murcia

♿ Excellent

✋ Moderate

28B4

✉ 55km north of Murcia

🍴 Choice of restaurants and bars (€–€€€)

🚌 From Murcia

Juan Carcelén Museo del Vino

✉ García Lorca 1

☎ 968 75 60 64 for apppointment

Museo Jerónimo Molina

✉ Plaza de la Constitución 3

☎ 968 78 07 40

🕐 Tue–Sat 9–1, 4–7, Sun 9–1

29D1

✉ 55km east of Murcia

🍴 Choice of restaurants and bars (€–€€€)

🚌 From Murcia

🚃 From Murcia

⛴ Excursions from Los Alcázares, Santiago de la Ribera and La Manga

Above: *La Manga's resort hotels provide accommodation for summer visitors from all over the world*

Left: *the tall shaft of the lighthouse at Cabo de Palos is visible from many points on the coast*

summer population of holiday-makers. The landward shore of the Mar saw some development in the 19th century when Spaniards from Murcia built spacious holiday homes at towns like Los Alcázares, San Javier and Santiago de la Ribera. These resorts are still Spanish favourites, with families returning year after year.

Cabo de Palos, at the southern end of La Manga on the seaward side, is the closest to a traditional village, a jolly fishing and sailing centre, known for its lighthouse, Sunday market and good fish restaurants. The Mar Menor covers 170sq km and is nowhere more than 7m deep, making it a perfect watersports centre. Sailing, windsurfing and water-skiing are all available, and frequent excursion boats visit the lagoon's five islands. The seaward side of La Manga has some excellent diving areas and further south along the coast there are quiet coves and beaches (➤ 83).

🛈 Mar Menor: Fuster 63, Los Alcázares ☎ 968 17 13 61; Padre Juan s/n, Santiago de la Ribera ☎ 968 57 17 04, km0 Las Amoladeras, La Manga del Mar Menor ☎ 968 14 61 36

♿ Few

❓ Hogueras de San Juan (24 Jun in San Pedro and San Javier), Virgen del Carmen (16 Jul in San Pedro, Santiago and Cabo de Palos)

↔ Calblanque (➤ 16)

87

Mula's Moorish castle dominates the narrow, traditional streets of this upland town

Did you know ?

One of the most extraordinary Holy Week customs in all Spain occurs in Mula and Moratalla, another upland town. For up to four days, these towns reverberate to continuous drumming, day and night, as the cloaked and hooded figures of hundreds of tambaradas *patrol the streets.*

➕ 28B1
✉️ 70km south of Murcia
🍴 Restaurants/bars (€–€€)
🚌 From Murcia
ℹ️ Avenida Doctor Meca 47 ☎ /fax 968 59 44 26
❓ Fallas de San José (12–20 Mar), Virgen del Carmen (16 Jul), Romería del Milagro de la Purísima (13–20 Nov)

➕ 28B2
✉️ 32km west of Murcia
🍴 Restaurants/bars (€–€€)
🚌 From Murcia
ℹ️ Convento de San Francisco, Calle Doña Elvira ☎ 968 66 15 01
♿ Few
❓ Semana Santa (Mar/Apr)
↔️ Sierra de Espuña (➤ 26)

MAZARRÓN ✪

Lead, silver, iron and zinc were mined in Mazarrón from earliest historical times by Carthaginians, Romans and Arabs. The mines have been worked out for years, but some of the handsome buildings erected from mining profits remain. Defensive towers, built against Berber pirate attacks, survive, though the castle of Los Veléz is in ruins. The Torres de los Caballos, next to the convent of La Purísima, and the Torre Vieja de la Cumbre are worth a look, as is the beautiful *mudéjar* panelling in the church of San Andres. Today the town and its port thrive on tomatoes, fishing and tourists. The harbour doubles as a sailing and diving centre, while along the coast runs a string of deserted coves and beaches (➤ 83).

MULA ✪✪

Situated by the Mula river, the town is packed with hidden delights and famed for its artisan traditions. Dominated by the 16th-century Castillo de los Veléz on the hill behind the town, the old quarter's narrow streets are scattered with fine buildings and churches, notably 16th-century Santo Domingo and San Miguel. The Museo del Cigarralejo is housed in a baroque mansion in the heart of town; its huge collection of Iberian art, excavated at a nearby necropolis, is one of Murcia's best. Within easy reach is the reservoir at La Cierva, and the little spa at Baños de Mula.

Into the Sierra de Espuña

Head northwest out of Alcantarilla on the C415, exit 651 from the Vía del Mediterráneo (E15).

You soon leave behind the light industry and built-up areas to drive through some of Murcia's fertile *huerta* (gardens), with acres of orange, almond and peach trees. As the road rises the vegetation thins and the mountains dramatically rise up to the west.

At Mula (➤ 88) turn left off the bypass on to the C3315 to Pliego.

Pliego is an historic town lying on one of the old transhumance routes. These ancient tracks, used until comparatively recently by shepherds to move stock from summer to winter pastures, criss-cross many Mediterranean regions.

After Pliego the road climbs steadily towards the village of Gevar. Once through the village look out after 6km for a right turning on to an unclassified road signposted Albergue Juvenil 8.5km.

This is the start of the route that climbs through the Sierra de Espuña (➤ 26), one of Spain's larger regional parks. This tortuous mountain road traverses the park through breathtaking mountain scenery, with wonderful viewpoints and good picnic places.

The road eventually drops down to join the MU503 at Aledo (➤ 84). Follow this to Totana (➤ 90). Then take the E15 motorway back to your start point at Alcantarilla.

Distance
120km

Time
4½ hours without stops, or a full day with visits

Start/end point
Alcantarilla
✚ 28C2

Lunch
Venta La Magdalena (€)
✉ Baños de Mula
☎ 968 66 05 68

The peak of Espuña towers above cool, fragrant pine forests

SEGURA VALLEY

The Moors were the first to irrigate the Segura valley, making it incredibly fertile; they planted orange, almond and fruit orchards, and remained here until the 17th century. Still lovely, despite the inevitable development, the valley includes diverse landscapes and a scatter of interesting towns and villages. North of the spa town of Archena, citrus groves predominate, and the valley narrows through a gorge before widening out at the historic town of Ojós. Further on, Ricote, with its brightly coloured houses, is worth a stop before continuing towards Blanca. One of Spain's largest water wheels is at nearby Abarán; first installed by the Moors, several of these immense wooden machines still function. North of here, peach orchards stretch in all directions, before the hills start to close in once more and the valley finally reaches Calasparra, famous for its rice.

Fruit orchards, orange groves and baroque architecture are typical sights in the Segura valley

TOTANA

Quickly reached down the motorway from Murcia, Totana lies on the edge of Murcia's splendid sierras, a good starting point for exploring the hill country. The town is mainly known for its pottery, made here since Moorish times. More than 20 potteries still function, producing an incredible range of ceramics, huge earthenware storage jars, pots and bowls. Some of these are still fired in the traditional Arab-style kiln, the *tosta*, where the pots stand on a perforated floor above the heat source. Workshops still produce the *cántara de Totana*, a traditional pitcher, probably first designed by the Romans. If you're shopping, head for the old pottery district in town, rather than the outlets aimed at the tourists along the main road.

Where To...

Above: *parasols are all important on the beach*
Right: *there are plenty of new experiences for children on the Costa Blanca*

Alicante (Alacant)

Prices

Prices are approximate, based on the cost of a three-course meal for one, without drinks or service.

€ = up to €6
€€ = €6–€15
€€€ = over €15

Eat Spanish

You will find a huge variety of different places, ranging from cheap and cheerful to restaurants whose style – and costs – rival top international restaurants anywhere. Those listed here mainly offer Spanish and local specialities, which might be more difficult to track down on your own. It is quite acceptable in Spain to have one course and a salad, so do not think you have to wade through the whole menu.

Azahar (€€)

The chef and maître d' from one of Alicante's oldest restaurants branched out here on their own, and the years of experience certainly show in the excellent cooking and attention to detail.

✉ C/ Alberola 57
☎ 965 12 13 48 🕐 Lunch and dinner. Closed Sun PM and Mon

El Bocaito (€€)

Atmospheric and lively bar and restaurant, serving *tapas* and a good range of dishes with the emphasis on rice and shellfish.

✉ Isabel la Católica 22
☎ 965 92 26 30 🕐 Lunch and dinner. Closed Sun

César Anca (€€)

A friendly pub-style restaurant, where the simple and appetising food is prepared with an up-to-date twist. Excellent service,, with more waiters in many much grander establishments.

✉ General Lacy 12
☎ 965 92 26 30 🕐 Closed Mon PM, Sun and all Jul

Los Charros (€)

A great lunch-time choice at the Playa de San Juan, this attractive bar-restaurant serves up the best tapas and traditional dishes among the bars in this part of town.

✉ Avenida de Bruselas 15
☎ 965 21 32 14 🕐 Lunch daily

Comino (€€)

Small and hidden-away restaurant with an intimate atmosphere and imaginative, subtle cooking, run by a husband-and-wife team. Good for a romantic evening.

✉ Segura 14 ☎ 965 21 32 14
🕐 Lunch and dinner. Closed Sun

Darsena (€€€)

An elegant restaurant in the Marina with the emphasis firmly on *arroces*, seafood and fish. Service can be a bit chaotic at busy times and the wine list can err towards fashion rather than quality

✉ Muelle de Levante 6, Marina Deportiva ☎ 965 20 75 89
🕐 Lunch and dinner. Closed Sun PM

Govana (€€)

A noisy, friendly restaurant where you can eat at the bar from the excellent *tapas* selection, or in the dining room choosing from more than 30 rice dishes.

✉ General Lacy 17 ☎ 965 92 56 58 🕐 Lunch and dinner. Closed Sun PM and Aug

Grill Sant Joan (€€€)

A hotel restaurant with a terrace. Many local dishes but Japanese specialities too. Wonderful service, excellent wine list.

✉ La Doblada s/n ☎ 965 16 13 00 🕐 Lunch and dinner

El Jardin de Galicia (€€)

Right in the heart of Alicante, specialising in traditional cooking from Galicia, from where much of the excellent meat and shellfish comes.

✉ Maisonnave 33 ☎ 965 12 01 61 🕐 Lunch and dinner. Closed Sun and 1–24 Jul

Jumillano (€€€)

This long-established *méson*-style restaurant began in the 1930s as a wine and oil shop – today it's one of Alicante's finest places to eat, serving impeccably cooked and presented local dishes.

✉ César Elguezábal 62
☎ 965 21 29 64 🕐 Closed Sun PM and Jul–Sep

Lo de Reme (€€)

A family restaurant with imaginative cooking; serving *bacalao*, dried cod, and liver and kidney dishes.

⊠ Isabel la Católica 6
☎ 965 12 39 02 🕒 Lunch and dinner. Closed Sun and Aug

El Lugar (€)

Good local cooking using the freshest ingredients; very good quality and value for money. Popular with locals.

⊠ García Morato 4
☎ 965 14 11 31 🕒 Lunch and dinner. Closed Sun and holidays

Maestral (€€)

An old-established upmarket restaurant, one of the first to open in the early tourist years, specialising in rice dishes and shellfish, as well as some international specialities.

⊠ Andalucía 18
☎ 965 16 46 18 🕒 Lunch and dinner. Closed Sun PM

Nou Manolin (€€)

Very popular bar and restaurant serving the best of Alicante and Spanish cooking. Rice and shellfish, with good wine list.

⊠ Villegas 3 ☎ 965 20 03 68
🕒 Lunch and dinner

One-One (€€)

Idiosyncratic restaurant with a French twist – no menus, just what looked good in the market that day, all served with panache and style.

⊠ Valdés 9 ☎ 965 20 63 99
🕒 Lunch and dinner. Closed Sun, holidays and Aug

Pachà (€€)

A good range of rice dishes, as well as braised meat and tasty fish, served in a traditional setting.

⊠ Haroldo Parrés 6
☎ 965 21 19 38 🕒 Lunch and dinner. Closed Wed

Pekin (€)

Peking-style cooking with the usual set meals or *à la carte*. Good downtown choice.

⊠ Reyes Católicos 57 ☎ 965 92 98 67 🕒 Lunch and dinner

Piripi (€€)

Rice cooked to perfection is the speciality in this friendly family-run restaurant. A huge range of *tapas* to start.

⊠ Oscar Esplá 30 ☎ 965 22 79 40 🕒 Lunch and dinner

Racó del Pla (€€)

Another excellent rice and fish restaurant, where the proprietors take pride in the freshness of all their ingredients. Pleasing décor, nice bar and good service.

⊠ Dr Nieto 42 ☎ 965 21 93 73
🕒 Lunch and dinner. Closed second two weeks in Aug

Tragallum (€€)

Recently opened restaurant where the chef makes full use of local ingredients and traditions; dishes include rabbit with pine-nuts and parsley, and fine terrines spiked with rosemary.

⊠ Campo Vassallo 33
☎ 965 21 38 69 🕒 Lunch and dinner. Closed Sun PM and Aug

Valencia 11 (€)

Wonderful-value bar-restaurant with a menu packed with Alicante dishes and some of the best puddings in town. Very popular, so it's best to book.

⊠ Valencia 11 ☎ 965 21 13 09
🕒 Lunch and dinner. Closed Sun and Mon PM, and mid-Aug to mid-Sep

Tapas

Tapas bars abound all over Spain, and are an excellent way to feel the spirit of a city. Don't be put off by dark interiors – these are often the best. You'll find them well patronised by locals having a quick snack with a glass of wine or beer. The dishes themselves range from olives and almonds, to *tortilla*, *jamón serrano*, shellfish, anchovies, meat croquettes and wonderful vegetable dishes, laced with chilli and garlic. The cold *tapas* are displayed at the counter and the hot ones cooked to order. *Raciones* are bigger servings than *porciones*; two or three will be plenty for lunch and a truly Spanish experience.

Around Alicante

Budget Eating
The resorts of the Costa Blanca have such a wide range of restaurants it's easy to find one to suit every pocket. For inexpensive eating you can head for a *tapas* bar or try the food on offer in a *cervecería* or *bodega*. These usually serve *platos combinados*, literally a combination plate, which should satisfy the healthiest appetite. One of these followed by a visit to a *heladería* (ice-cream bar) provides a good simple meal.

Benifallím
El Celler (€€)
A country restaurant in the foothills of the Sierra de Aitana with local game-based dishes. Not much to look at but friendly, and you'll find specialities not available in the towns.

☒ Carrer Nou 1 ☎ 965 51 32 65 ⏰ Lunch and dinner in summer, lunch only in winter except Fri and Sat. Closed Mon

Elche (Elx)
Asador Ilicitano (€€)
If Valencian fare is beginning to pall, head for this rustic-style restaurant for a taste of Castile – huge roasts (including suckling pig), hearty bean dishes and fine hams, as well as fish dishes.

☒ Maestro Giner 9 ☎ 965 43 58 64 ⏰ Lunch and dinner. Closed Sun and 2 weeks in Aug

Doña Ana (€)
Come to this bastion of traditional cooking to enjoy succulent grilled meats, fish and shellfish. On weekdays they also offer a good-value *menú del día*.

☒ Dr Caro 17 ☎ 965 44 44 94 ⏰ Lunch and dinner. Closed Sun PM

La Finca (€€€)
Good grills, fish and game dishes and a terrace for summer eating. Much-patronised by local businessmen; service can be slow, however.

☒ Partida Perleta 1 ☎ 965 45 60 07 ⏰ Lunch and dinner. Closed Sun PM and three weeks in Jan

Parque Municipal (€)
Big and busy restaurant in the centre of Elche's magnificent palm forest.

The décor is functional but the food spot-on; a good place to eat *arroz con costra*.

☒ Paseo Estación s/n ☎ 965 45 34 15 ⏰ Lunch and dinner

Guardamar del Segura
Rincón de Pedro (€)
A perfect choice for holiday-makers with a cheerful, lively atmosphere, big terrace and good range of traditional rice and fish dishes.

☒ Cibeles 2, Urbanización las Dunas ☎ 965 72 80 95 ⏰ Lunch and dinner. Closed Wed in winter

Monóvar (Monòver)
Casa Elias (€€)
This is a good place to sample some of the inland rice dishes and traditional, country-style home cooking.

☒ Rosales 7, Cinorlet ☎ 966 97 95 17 ⏰ Lunch only

Xiri (€€)
The food has character and uses fresh local ingredients in its range of rice and pasta dishes. Excellent selection of the best of the local wines.

☒ Parque Alameda s/n ☎ 965 47 29 10 ⏰ Lunch and dinner. Closed Sun PM, Mon and 20 Feb–15 Mar

Orihuela
Los Barriles (€€)
An old tavern renowned for the excellent quality of the ingredients used in its fish, shellfish and rice dishes. You also have the choice of eating at the bar which has a good selection of interesting *tapas*.

☒ La Sal 1 ☎ 966 74 23 65 ⏰ Lunch and dinner. Closed Sun and Aug

Casa Corro (€)

Functional, but excellent restaurant near Orihuela's palm forest, with the accent on regional cooking.

✉ Avenida García Rogel s/n, Palmeral de San Antón ☎ 965 30 29 63 🍴 Lunch and dinner. Closed Mon PM and second two weeks of Aug

Santa Pola
Batiste (€€)

A very pretty restaurant, situated in a flower-filled garden right beside the sea, offering shellfish, rice and fish, and an excellent wine list.

✉ Pérez Ojeda 6 ☎ 965 41 14 85 🍴 Lunch and dinner

La Goleta (€€)

A nautically themed tavern offering great rice recipes from the island of Tabarca. The fish and shellfish are wonderfully fresh and there is a lively atmosphere.

✉ Hernán Cortés 6 ☎ 966 69 30 63 🍴 Lunch and dinner. Closed Mon (except Jul and Aug), and two weeks in Oct/Nov

Miramar (€€)

An elegant summer restaurant with a big terrace and friendly service. Local rice and fish, with lots of vegetables and the freshest of salads.

✉ Pérez Ojeda 8 ☎ 965 41 10 00 🍴 Lunch and dinner. Closed Sun PM from Oct–Jun

Palomar (€€)

Enjoy the best of local rice and seafood dishes right beside the beach on the terrace of this bustling restaurant.

✉ Playa de Levante s/n ☎ 965 41 32 00 🍴 Lunch and dinner

Rincón de Rafa (€€)

Rafa's is housed in an old private house, with a series of private dining rooms where you can savour light, Mediterranean-style cooking.

✉ C/ Poeta Miguel Hernández 15 ☎ 965 69 10 02 🍴 Lunch and dinner. Closed Sun PM

Torrevieja
Bahía (€)

Good range of seafood and international dishes in this popular tourist restaurant.

✉ Avenida Libertad 3 ☎ 965 71 39 94 🍴 Lunch and dinner

Brisas del Mar (€)

Popular restaurant with terrace; some unusual local dishes such as caldero.

✉ Paseo Vista Alegre 10 ☎ 965 70 52 01 🍴 Lunch and dinner. Closed Mon PM

Buffet las Salinas (€)

Super-value self-service restaurant. Over 70 dishes; rice, fish, roast meat and salads.

✉ C/ Ramón Galud 173 ☎ No telephone 🍴 Lunch and dinner. Closed Jan and Sun PM

Cabo Roig (€€)

Pleasantly situated restaurant on Cabo Roig, with a large summer terrace.

✉ Urbanización Cabo Roig s/n, Carretera Torrevieja–Cartagena Km 8 ☎ 966 76 02 90 🍴 Lunch and dinner

Villena
Wary Nessy (€)

Excellent family-run restaurant specialising in dishes peculiar to Villena; bar food and good local wines.

✉ Isabel la Católica 13A ☎ 965 80 10 47 🍴 Lunch and dinner. Closed Mon and second two weeks in Jul

Vegetarian Eating

Although Spaniards do not really understand vegetarianism, if you eat fish you will find possibilities on every menu. If not, the range of vegetable dishes available is huge, particularly in Murcia. Salads appear everywhere and it is quite acceptable to ask for a tortilla, the classic potato and onion omelette. Country places often have wonderful local vegetable stews and soups, cheese is good and some rice dishes have no meat or fish in them. If you are staying in the Benidorm area, an excellent vegetarian restaurant is The Olive Tree in Camino del Paelleio in Moraira, which has a wide range of choices, and meat and fish dishes as well.

Benidorm & the North

Venturing Forth

The chances are your holiday price will include three meals a day, but make a point of splashing out on one or two restaurant meals to ensure you sample some really local dishes. By law, restaurants offer a three-course *menu del día* (menu of the day), which will often feature rice and fish dishes and be generally good value. The smaller the restaurant the higher the chance of finding real Spanish food; the buzz of Spanish voices will tell you if you're on the right track. Many menus feature illustrations of the various specialities, so you should not have a language problem.

Benidorm

L'Albufera (€)

This popular restaurant is busy all day, thanks to the great range of *tapas*, good-value *menús*.and splendid rice dishes.

✉ Gerona 3 ☎ 965 86 56 61
🕓 Lunch and dinner

La Palmera-Casa Paco Nadal (€€)

One of Benidorm's oldest restaurants, with a pretty terrace, specialising in fish and rice dishes.

✉ Avenida Dr Severo Ochoa 44, Rincón de Loix
☎ 965 85 32 82
🕓 Lunch only except Jul–Aug

El Pulpo Pirata (€)

A restaurant and bar near the old quarter popular with local people. Good range of excellent-value dishes and *tapas* and a tiny shady terrace for eating alfresco.

✉ Calle Tomás Ortuño s/n
☎ 966 80 32 19
🕓 Lunch and dinner

Rías Baixas (€€)

Grab a terrace table at this big, functional restaurant where you can sample plain grilled fish, excellent shellfish and some more international dishes at excellent prices.

✉ Plaza Torrechó 3 ☎ 965 85 50 22 🕓 Lunch and dinner

Altea

Ca Toni (€€)

Welcoming and elegant restaurant serving local produce with a light approach. Interesting wine list and an outdoor terrace.

✉ Rector Llinares 3, La Vela
☎ 965 84 34 97 🕓 Lunch and dinner. Closed Wed except 15 Jul–1 Sep

Montemolar (€€€)

Upmarket and slightly ostentatious but elegant restaurant. Fine fresh produce, caviar, scottish salmon and fillet steak.

✉ Monte Molar 38
☎ 965 84 15 81 🕓 Dinner only. Closed Wed and Jan–Mar

El Patio (€€)

There's a cool shady garden at this good local eatery where the specialities include *paella, fideuà, arroz a la banda* and the freshest of plain grilled fish.

✉ Avenida del Puerto 9
☎ 965 84 39 89 🕓 Lunch and dinner. Closed Nov–Feb

Cabo de la Nao (Cap de la Nau)

Cabo la Nau (€€)

Beautifully situated restaurant perched on a high headland with splendid views. Good *tapas*, rice and fish and a pretty outside terrace to eat on.

✉ Faro Cabo de la Nau, Jávea
☎ 965 77 18 35
🕓 Lunch and dinner

Calpe (Calp)

Casa Florencia (€€)

Tucked away in one of the most attractive corners of old Calpe, this pretty restaurant serves good Valencian cooking with the accent on rice and fish.

✉ Plaça del Mariners
☎ 965 83 35 84 🕓 Lunch and dinner. Closed Sun PM

Internacional (€€)

Set right on the beach, the Internacional has a big airy dining room and a splendid terrace; choose from the à la carte menu or good-value *menú del día* – any time from 9AM to midnight.

☒ Edificio Aguamarina, Playa de Levante ☎ 965 83 60 03 ⊙ Lunch and dinner. Closed Jan and Feb

Dénia
El Asador del Puerto (€€)
Classic eating house where the accent is firmly on meat, including game in season.
☎ 966 42 34 82 ⊙ Lunch and dinner. Closed Wed, except May–Sep

El Raset (€€€)
One of Dénia's oldest and smartest restaurants, in a pretty old building in the fishing quarter.
☒ Bellaviata 7 ☎ 965 78 50 40 ⊙ Lunch and dinner. Tue except in Jul and Sep

Gandía
Emilio (€€)
Sophisticated restaurant near the beach. Great use is made of fresh market produce; a good choice for something a bit special.
☒ B Bloque F-5, Avda, Vicente Calderón ☎ 962 84 07 61 ⊙ Lunch and dinner. Cosed Wed except Jul and Aug

Guadalest
Venta la Montaña (€€)
An old inn with a terrace, opened in 1910, and still going strong. Dishes typical of this area slightly away from the coast.
☒ Carretera Alcoy 9, Benimantell ☎ 965 88 51 41 ⊙ Lunch and dinner in summer, dinner only in winter. Closed Mon except in Aug

Játiva (Xàtiva)
Casa la Abuela (€€€)
Excellent restaurant offering traditional local recipes; look out for *arnadí*, a rich dessert cake made with pumpkin, almonds and pine-nuts.
☒ Reina 17 ☎ 962 28 10 85 ⊙ Lunch and dinner. Closed Sun, and mid-Jun to mid Aug

Jávea (Xàbia)
Tasca Tonis (€)
The locals' favourite, so it's busy year-round. Home-cooking at its best, using local ingredients. There's a different 'special' every day .
☒ Mayor 4 ☎ 962 46 18 51 ⊙ Lunch and dinner. Closed Sun PM

Moraira
Girasol (€€€)
A pretty chalet with a terrace considered the foremost restaurant in Valencia and one of the best in Spain.
☒ Carretera Moraira–Calpe Km 1.5 ☎ 966 74 43 73 ⊙ Lunch and dinner. Closed Mon, except in summer, and Nov

La Seu (€)
Imaginative Valencian cooking at half the price of the Girasol up the road.
☒ Dr Calatayud 24 ☎ 965 74 57 52 ⊙ Lunch and dinner. Closed Tue

Sella
Bar Fonda (€)
Serving good country dishes, this is popular with locals, so it's best to book in advance.
☒ Carretera Alcoy 15 ☎ 965 87 90 11 ⊙ Lunch and dinner

Villajoyosa (La Vila Joiosa)
Casa Elordi (€€)
A pretty old house in the historic quarter. Head for the palm-shaded terrace.
☒ Puerta Dr Esquerdo 8 ☎ 966 85 26 63 ⊙ Lunch and dinner. Closed Sun and Mon

Arroz
Arroz, or rice, is the staple in this area, and is found up and down the Costa Blanca. It grows all over the region, but the most famous comes from the inland town of Calasparra, high in the Segura valley, and is one of Spain's few foods with a *denominación de origen*. Spanish rice has a nutty, intense flavour and a good bite even when cooked. To taste it at its best it must be served as soon as it is cooked, steaming and aromatic with the fish, meat and vegetables that flavour it. To enjoy the real thing, sample it in a restaurant that specialises in *arroces*, and make sure the menu advises a 20-minute wait – the time it takes to cook rice to perfection.

Murcia

The *Huerta*

Look on any pack of vegetables in your supermarket at home, and the chances are high that the producer's address will be in Murcia. The fertile flatlands, the *huerta* (garden), around the city was first cultivated by the Moors and has produced intensely flavoured, tender young vegetables and a range of fruit for centuries. With the advent of rapid refrigerated transport, the industry boomed and today the *huerta* supplies many northern European markets. Much produce still stays at home, though, providing the raw ingredients for the huge range of delicious and imaginative vegetable dishes that are an essential part of Murcian cooking.

Murcia

El Churra (€)

A pretty restaurant serving classic Murcian recipes, offering a wide range of local vegetable specialities, plus excellent grilled steaks and a comprehensive wine list.

✉ Avenida Marqués de los Vélez 12 ☎ 968 23 84 00
🍽 Lunch and dinner

El Felipe (€€)

Genuine Murcian vegetable and egg-based specialities at reasonable prices, as well as meat and fish, at this friendly restaurant across the river from the cathedral.

✉ C/ González Adalid 11
☎ 968 21 20 66 🍽 Lunch and dinner. Closed Sun PM and Aug

Hispano (€€)

Murcian-style restaurant, with outstanding vegetable dishes and excellent fish. Good wine list and attentive service.

✉ Radio Murcia 3 ☎ 968 21 61 52 🍽 Lunch and dinner. Closed Sat in Jul and Aug

Mesón el Corral (€€)

Right in the heart of the old town and decorated with hand-painted *azulejos*, this friendly restaurant offers an enormous range of *tapas* as well as a full menu.

✉ Plaza Santo Domingo 23–24
☎ 968 21 45 97/21 49 85
🍽 Lunch and dinner

La Onda (€€)

A cool and elegant restaurant near all the main sites, serving fish and meat dishes and Murcian vegetable specialities. Range of wines.

✉ Bando de la Huerta 8
☎ 968 24 78 82 🍽 Lunch and dinner. Closed Sun and 10 days in Aug

Rincón del Pepe (€€€)

The restaurant that put traditional Murcian cooking firmly on the Spanish gastronomic map. Wonderful local vegetable, meat and fish dishes and a superb wine selection.

✉ Apóstoles 34 ☎ 968 21 22 39 🍽 Lunch and dinner

Rocío (€)

Restaurant on the edge of the historic centre started by two chefs formerly at the famous Rincón del Pepe (above), serving similar Murcian dishes at half the price. Worth seeking out.

✉ Batalla de las Flores s/n
☎ 968 24 29 30 🍽 Lunch and dinner. Closed Sun

Águilas

Las Brisas (€€)

Maritime-themed restaurant serving fresh fish and rice dishes – try the huge prawns, crayfish or light-as-a-feather *fritura de pascado*.

✉ Explanda del Puerto s/n
☎ 968 41 00 27
🍽 Lunch and dinner

El Algar

Los Churrascos (€€)

One of the region's best restaurants, rustically decorated. Superb meat and fish; renowned wine list.

✉ Avenida Filipinas 13
☎ 968 13 61 44
🍽 Lunch and dinner

Cabo de Palos

Miramar (€€)

Big functional restaurant in a wonderful position beside the sea, renowned for its freshest of fish and lightest of frying.

✉ Paeso de la Barra 14
☎ 968 56 30 33 🍽 Lunch and dinner. Closed Tue and Jan

El Mosqui (€€)

Housed in a building resembling an upturned boat and noted for its rice and fish; busy weekends.

🖂 Subida al Faro 50 ☎ 968 56 45 63 🕔 Lunch and dinner, weekends only in low season

Caravaca de la Cruz
Los Viñales (€)

Inland Murcian cooking in this unpretentious spacious restaurant. Excellent meat dishes, good vegetables, and cheese tart for pudding. Local wines only.

🖂 Avenida Juan Carlos I 41 ☎ 968 70 84 58 🕔 Lunch and dinner. Closed Tue and for two weeks in Oct

Cartagena
Mare Nostrum (€€)

Low-key but elegant restaurant with the best sea views in town. Beautifully cooked local dishes, mainly fish and vegetables.

🖂 Puerto Alfonso XII, Puerto Deportivo ☎ 968 52 21 31 🕔 Lunch and dinner

Jumilla
Monasterio (€)

A large restaurant on the town outskirts. Functional with excellent food; a Spanish experience.

🖂 Avenida de la Asunción 40 ☎ 968 78 20 92 🕔 Lunch and dinner. Closed Tue

La Manga del Mar Menor
Amapola (€€)

Even if you're not staying at the Hyatt Club you can eat at this elegant restaurant. Local ingredients with an international twist.

🖂 Hyatt La Manga Club Resort, Los Belones ☎ 968 13 72 34 🕔 Lunch and dinner

Borsalino (€)

If you feel like a change from Spanish dishes this is a good place to eat; French dishes appear alongside local specialities such as fish baked in salt. Fine wine list.

🖂 Edificio Babylonia ☎ 968 56 31 30 🕔 Lunch and dinner. Closed Tue in winter and 7 Jan to 12 Feb

Mula
Venta La Magdalena (€)

First-rate upcountry cooking using the freshest ingredients in simple surroundings, with plenty of locals eating. Excellent rabbit and rice dishes; house wine.

🖂 Baños de Mula ☎ 968 66 05 68 🕔 Lunch and dinner. Closed on Wed and from 15 Jul–15 Aug

Puerto de Mazarrón
Virgen del Mar (€)

Agreeable local restaurant; go for the shellfish or fish dishes and enjoy the friendly service and relaxed atmosphere.

🖂 Paseo Marítimo s/n ☎ 968 59 50 57 🕔 Lunch only

San Pedro del Pinatar
Juan Mari (€€)

Probably the best restaurant on this stretch of the coast with locally cured hams, super-fresh shellfish and imaginative puddings.

🖂 Alcalde Julio Albaladejo 12 ☎ 968 18 38 69 🕔 Lunch and dinner. Closed Mon low season

Totana
Venta de la Rata (€€)

Friendly and locally loved restaurant specialising in every combination of rice, meat, fish and vegetables. Often busy at weekends.

🖂 Ctra de la Santa s/n ☎ 968 42 17 04 🕔 Lunch and dinner

Healthy Eating

On a Spanish holiday it's not just the sun and relaxation that does you good, it's also what you eat. A traditional Spanish diet is not only delicious but healthy. Good bread, olive oil, fish, large quantities of fresh fruit and vegetables are the staples, with meat, dairy produce and sweet things in just the right quantity. Spaniards drink little alcohol and lots of water, ideal in the high summer temperatures.

99

Alicante & Around

Prices

Prices are for a double room, excluding breakfast and IVA, the Spanish equivalent of VAT.

€ = under €30
€€ = €30–60
€€€ = over €60

Hotel Gradings

Officially registered hotels in Spain range from one to five stars (with an additional top de luxe category of GL, Gran Lujo). Other types of accommodation include apartment hotels, hotel residences (no restaurant), hostels and pensions. Stars are assigned according to service and facilities available. Suites can usually be found in the four- or five-star range. Tariffs should be displayed by law.

Alicante (Alacant)

Almirante (€€)

Right on the seafront at San Juan, this is an ideal choice for windsurfing and watersports enthusiasts. Good restaurant, friendly staff and tranquillity.

☒ Avenida Niza 38 ☎ 965 65 01 12; www.hotelalmirante.com

Castilla Alicante (€€)

Comfortable, modern, well-equipped hotel, set one block back from the beach at San Juan. Good-sized rooms all with balcony; there's a pool, shady palms, and full bar and restaurant service.

☒ Avenida Países Escandinavos 7 ☎ 965 16 20 33; www.hcastilla.com

Covadonga (€)

A good central air-conditioned choice with parking and a garage, which often has room when other hotels are full. Ask for one of the quieter interior rooms.

☒ Plaza de los Luceros 17 ☎ 965 20 28 44

Mediterránea Plaza (€€€)

Stylish, comfortable hotel in the centre of the old town, facing the Ayuntamiento and a stone's throw from the sea – there are lovely views of the old quarter and the castle from virtually every room.

☒ Pl de Ayuntamiento 6 ☎ 965 21 01 88; www.hotelmediterraneaplaza.com

les Monges (€)

This friendly, family-run budget hotel is housed in a pleasant, recently renovated turn-of-the-century building right in the centre of town.

☒ Monges 2–1 ☎ 965 21 50 46

Rambla 9 (€)

Convenient, centrally situated budget hotel with nice rooms and air-conditioning, on a wide avenue leading to the sea.

☒ Rambla Méndez Núñez 9 ☎ 965 14 45 80

Sidi San Juan (€€€)

The ultimate in resort hotels a little north of the city centre. Lovely views, every comfort, three pools and access to the beach through the manicured grounds.

☒ La Doblada s/n, Playa de San Juan ☎ 965 16 13 00; www.hotelsidi.es

Alcoy (Alcoi)

Mas de Pau (€)

This beautifully restored 18th-century granary stands in lovely country 9km east of Alcoy with superb views. Rather small rooms, but worth it for the restaurant, pool and ambience.

☒ Carretera Alcoy-Penáguila, Km 9 ☎ 965 51 31 09

Biar

Villa de Biar (€)

Delightful hotel in a historic town, with elegant public rooms and lovely views. It incorporates the palace of the viscounts of Valdesoto.

☒ San José 2 ☎ 965 81 13 04; e-mail: hotelbiar@ctv.es

Elche (Elx)

Candelijas (€)

A good, family-run budget choice in the centre of town with clean, well-equipped rooms, all with bathrooms, air-conditioning and a lift.

☒ Doctor Ferrán 19 ☎ 965 46 65 12

Huerto del Cura (€€€)

A luxurious and traditional

hotel, affiliated to the state *paradors*, set in the middle of Elche's palm groves and opposite the famous garden. Lovely grounds, every facility and an excellent restaurant.

🖂 **Porta de la Morera 14**
☎ **966 61 00 11;**
www.huertodelcura.com

Guardamar
Edén Mar (€)
Summer season, excellent budget hotel. Near the beach, within easy walk of bars and restaurants and all rooms have bathrooms.

🖂 **Avenida Mediterráneo 19**
☎ **965 72 92 13**

Meridional (€€)
Pleasant holiday hotel, right on the beach, which had a complete overhaul in 2001. No pool, but tennis, satellite TV and friendly staff.

🖂 **Urbanización Dunas de Guardamar** ☎ **965 72 83 40;**
hotel meridional.es

Orihuela
SH Palacio de Tudemir (€€€)
Lovely hotel housed in a beautifully restored 18th-century palace in the historic heart of Orihuela (opened 2001). Facilities and service in keeping with a hotel of this calibre – even a sauna.

🖂 **Alfonso XIII 1** ☎ **965 73 80 10; e-mail: palaciotudemir@sh-serotel.com**

Santa Pola
Marina Palace (€€)
Well-appointed modern hotel, with pool, large rooms and excellent restaurant, located only ten minutes from Alicante airport.

🖂 **Carretera Alicante-Cartagena Km 17** ☎ **965 41 13 12;**
www.hotelmarinapalace.com

Pola-Mar (€€)
Large hotel, right on the seafront next to the port and sailing club. Popular with Spanish families; good restaurant and lovely views.

🖂 **Playa de Levante 6**
☎ **965 41 32 00;**
e-mail: info@polamar.com

Tabarca
Casa del Gobernador (€)
A wonderful hotel in the restored 18th-century governor's house in Tabarca, with cool, lofty rooms.

🖂 **Azhar 20 s/n, Isla de Tabarca** ☎ **965 96 08 86;**
www.casadelgobernador.com

Torrevieja
Lloyds Club (€€)
An apartment hotel with a restaurant and pool in a superb beach-side position. Tastefully furnished and well-equipped apartments, each with its own kitchen and a terrace overlooking the sea.

🖂 **Avenida de los Holandeses 2** ☎ **966 92 00 00**

Masa Internacional (€€)
On a promontory overlooking the sea, with superb views; this pretty and comfortable hotel, a little outside town, would suit people wanting to escape Torrevieja's frenetic summer evenings.

🖂 **Avenida Alfredo Nobel 150**
☎ **966 92 15 37; e-mail: hotel-masa@arrakis.com**

Villena
Salvadora (€)
An old-fashioned hotel, with better facilities than its one-star rating would imply. Excellent restaurant specialising in local dishes.

🖂 **Avenida de la Constitución 102** ☎ **965 80 09 50; www.hotel salvadora.com**

Value for Money
Many visitors to the Costa Blanca stay in beach hotels in the main resorts. Taken as part of a package tour, such accommodation offers excellent value for money. But seaside hotels tend to be expensive when booked independently. Remember that inland hotels are generally much cheaper, with a level of service and facilities of a higher standard than those at the same price in the big resorts. Whether or not you hire a car, a night away won't wreck the holiday budget and will give you a chance to explore further from base.

Benidorm & the North

Travellers with Disabilities

Facilities for travellers with disabilities are gradually improving on the Costa Blanca, though progress is far from fast. An increasing number of hotels do have good access for wheelchairs, wide lifts and doorways, and easy parking, though ground-floor rooms are few and far between. Blue Flag beaches have ramps down to the actual beach, but getting around inland villages is not always easy. If you have special needs contact your tour operator or the hotel in advance. For further information for visitors with disabilities get in touch with:

Direccion Territorial de Turismo ✉ **Calle Churruca 29, 03003 Alicante**
☎ **965 90 08 00**

Benidorm

Agir (€€)
A long-established hotel on Benidorm's main avenue, which was entirely renovated in 1997.
✉ **Avenida Mediterráneo 11**
☎ **965 85 51 62;**
www.hotelagir.com

Bristol Park (€€€)
Housed in a traditional-style building, and fairly small, but offering the full range of services including a pool.
✉ **C / Doctor Fleming** ☎ **965 85 14 482; www.onasol.es**

Climbel (€€)
One of Benidorm's most traditional hotels, right next to the Playa de Levante, with a pool and air-conditioning.
✉ **Avenida Europa 1** ☎ **965 85 21 00; www.hotelclimbel.com**

Fleming (€)
Good-value, typically Spanish family-run holiday hotel, near both beach and town centre, with a pool and some garden – a bonus in this price range.
✉ **Maravall 11**
☎ **965 85 32 62**

Gran Hotel Delfín (€€)
At the far end of the Playa de Poniente in an oasis of sub-tropical gardens, with good service and clean rooms. (Closed Nov to mid-March.)
✉ **Av Mont Benidorm 13**
☎ **965 85 34 00;**
www.webic/granhotel-delfin

Sol Pelicanos Ocas (€€)
Four pools, tennis courts and close to beach; ideal for families looking for style and comfort. All rooms have bathrooms and balconies; entertainment for all ages.
✉ **Gerona 45–47** ☎ **965 85 23 50; www.solmelia.com**

Altea

Alataya (€€)
Long-established hotel totally renovated in 2000, over-looking the seaside *paseo*. Big, comfortable rooms with sea views, and with a good restaurant.
✉ **Sant Pere 28** ☎ **965 84 08 00; e-mail: altaya@erasmus.com**

Calpe (Calp)

Galetamar (€€)
Modern, well-equipped hotel with balconies, sea views, good-size pool and spacious lounge areas. Accommodation includes family rooms and individual bungalows.
✉ **La Caleta 28** ☎ **965 83 23 11; www.galetamar.com**

Venta La Chata (€)
A family-run hotel in a 200-year-old country house in the countryside between Calpe and Benissa, with views to the mountains and the sea.
✉ **Carretera N-332 Km 172**
☎ **965 83 03 08**

Cocentaina

Els Frares (€)
A tiny hotel well outside the town in an elegantly restored old house, located in a mountain village with wonderful views. Peaceful and quiet, a warm welcome and interesting cooking.
✉ **Avenida del País Valencia, Quatretondeta** ☎ **965 51 12 34; www.mountainwalks.com**

Dénia

Los Angeles (€€€)
A pleasant resort hotel with direct access to the beach, a little north of Dénia in the busy Les Marines area.
✉ **Playa de Les Marines Km 4**
☎ **965 78 04 58; www.hotel losangelesdenia.com**

Buenavista (€€€)

Surrounded by pine trees, this small and lovely hotel, with pool, is housed in a skilfully converted 19th-century mansion. The restaurant accents local dishes and ingredients.

✉ **Partida Tossalet 82**
☎ **965 78 79 95;**
www.hotel-buenavista.com

Gandía

Bayren 1 (€€)

A classic seaside hotel situated right on the beach front, with all facilities and within a short walk's distance of all the resort's major attractions.

✉ **Paseo Neptuno 62–623**
☎ **962 84 03 00;**
www.hotelesbayren.com

Borgia (€€)

A hotel not purely aimed at holiday makers, near the town centre, with good-sized rooms at reasonable rates.

✉ **República Argentina 5**
☎ **962 87 81 09;**
e-mail: hborgia@wanadoo.es

Riviera (€)

Pleasant family-run beach hotel on the *paseo marítimo* with clean functional rooms, all with sea-facing balcony. Friendly service and good restaurant. Shut in winter.

✉ **Paseo Marítimo de Neptuno 28** ☎ **962 84 00 66**

Guadalest

El Trestellador (€)

A small family-run mountain hotel high in the Guadalest valley. Simple comfortable rooms, fine views and excellent local cooking.

✉ **Partida del Trestellador, Benimantell**
☎ **965 88 52 21; e-mail:**
eltrestellador@netvision.es

Játiva (Xàtiva)

Hostería de Mont Sant (€€)

An elegant and historic country house hotel in a wonderful situation on the hillside above the town and below the castle. Lovely gardens, pool, superb views and the service is friendly.

✉ **Carretera del Castillo s/n**
☎ **962 27 50 81;**
www.servidex.com/monsant

Jávea (Xàbia)

Parador de Jávea (€€€)

The only *parador* on the Costa Blanca, the de Jávea is a modern, luxury hotel beautifully situated in verdant gardens. There is direct beach access and a very high level of service and comfort.

✉ **Mediterráneo 7** ☎ **965 70 93 08; www.parador.es**

Moraira

Swiss Moraira (€€)

A relatively small hotel, the Swiss Moraira is set back from the sea in a beautiful valley and offers a high level of comfort and tranquillity. All the facilities you would expect to find, including a swimming pool and tennis court.

✉ **Haya 175, Urbanizacion Club Moraira** ☎ **965 74 71 04**

Villajoyosa (La Vila Joiosa)

El Montíboli (€€€)

Justifiably described in its publicity material as 'a corner of paradise', this luxury hotel is set on a promontory above two secluded bays and backed by hills. It is equally renowned for its superb restaurants.

✉ **Partida Montíboli s/n**
☎ **965 89 02 50;**
www.servigroup.es

Self-catering

Renting a villa or flat, whether it's on the coast or in some tranquil rural backwater, gives you much more freedom of choice than an 'all-inclusive' stay. Freedom to eat what you want when you want, to spread yourself out, not to worry about your children's excitement, to wear what you want, to go to bed and get up when you like. Then there's the added pleasure of trying different bars and restaurants for dinner, or shopping at the market and cooking something good at home. You can book such accommodation as part of a flight-inclusive holiday, or directly through the owners and their agents throughout the region. Local tourist offices have lists of self-catering options available by post or fax.

Murcia

Living like the Spanish
If you decide to tour around and stay in inland towns and villages, you may find things a little different from the international standards of the coast. Modest country hotels will tend to have showers rather than baths and no air-conditioning, so keep the shutters closed during the heat of the day. Eating is more geared to local habits, so lunch and dinner are late.

Murcia

Arco de San Juan (€€)
One of the city's great hotels, situated in Murcia's historic centre. Tasteful and comfortable, hidden behind an 18th-century façade, with a high level of friendly and professional service.
☒ Plaza Ceballos 10 ☎ 968 21 04 55; www.arcosanjuan.com

Casa Emilio (€)
A good budget choice with clean and comfortable rooms, this small hotel lies across the river within 10 minutes' walk of the historic centre.
☒ Alameda de Colón 9
☎ 968 22 06 31

Hispano II (€)
A traditional Murcian hotel, right in the historic centre and near the cathedral and main shops, with good service and comfortable rooms.
☒ Radio Murcia 3
☎ 968 21 61 52;
www.ono.com/hotelhispano

Águilas

Al Sur (€€)
It's worth driving out of Aguilas to reach this Mediterranean-style hotel, wonderfully situated on a promontory with great sea views, friendly proprietors and a laid-back atmosphere.
☒ Torre de Copa 24, Calabardina ☎ 968 41 94 66

Carlos III (€€)
A small hotel in the bustling centre of town, professionally and courteously run, with comfortable rooms.
☒ Avenida Carlos III 22
☎ 968 41 16 50;
www.hotelcarlosiii.com

Cabo de Palos

El Cortijo (€)
A family-run hotel in this atmospheric fishing village with clean, simple rooms.
☒ Calas 6, Subida al Faro s/n
☎ 968 56 30 15

Caravaca de la Cruz

Central (€)
A good base for exploring the Segura valley, this small country town hotel, with comfortable rooms and friendly service, will give a real taste of inland Spain.
☒ Gran Vía 18 ☎ 968 70 70 55

El Molino del Río (€)
A converted 16th-century mill in a truly rural setting in the undiscovered hinterland, high in the Argos valley system. A mixture of self-catering and hotel-type accommodation; the mill has its own restaurant and pool.
☒ Camoni Viejo de Archivel
☎ 606 30 14 09;
www.molinodelrio.com

Cartagena

Alfonso XIII (€€)
Cartagena's main central hotel, a large classical building with spacious rooms and elegant architectural details. High level of service.
☒ Paseo Alfonso XIII 40
☎ 968 52 00 00;
www.hotelalfonsoxiii.com

Los Habaneros (€)
A good place to stay on the outskirts of the city, with parking. Particularly well-known for its restaurant.
☒ San Diego 60
☎ 968 50 52 50

Fortuna

Balneario (€)
A wonderful Edwardian spa hotel with sweeping

staircases and lofty public rooms. The pool is fed by the hot springs and the hotel basement contains the treatment rooms.

✉ Balneario s/n
☎ 968 68 50 11; www.leana.es

La Manga del Mar Menor
La Cavanna (€€)
This vast hotel, overlooking the Mar Menor, has every conceivable facility for holiday-makers and is a short walk from all the attractions.

✉ Plaza Cavanna s/n ☎ 968 56 36 00; www.entramares.com

Dos Mares (€)
A small hotel right in the middle of the action. Clean and functional, it is excellent value for money.

✉ Plaza Bohemia s/n
☎ 968 14 00 93

Hyatt Regency La Manga (€€€)
Murcia's only five-star hotel, with its own golf course and a country-club atmosphere. Superb service, along with an excellent restaurant, tennis facilities and a pool.

✉ Los Belones ☎ 968 33 12 34; www.lamanga.hyatt.com

Sol Galúa (€€€)
This modern resort hotel, right near the sea, offers big, comfortable rooms, spacious lounge and public areas and all facilities including 24-hour room service

✉ Hacienda Dos Mares ☎ 968 56 32 00; www.solmelia.com

Villas La Manga (€€)
A well-run hotel in the heart of the resort's strip of development, with tastefully decorated rooms, excellent service and a pool.

✉ Gran Viá de la Manga s/n
☎ 968 14 52 22;
www.villaslamanga.es

Puerto de Mazarrón
Bahía (€)
A medium-sized hotel right on the seafront. Simple décor and friendly staff.

✉ Playa de la Reya s/n
☎ 968 59 40 00;
www.hotelbahia.com

La Cumbre (€)
Truly a hotel with a view; conventional but comfortable rooms, friendly staff and acceptable food.

✉ Urbanización La Cumbre
☎ 968 59 48 61

Mula
Alcázar (€)
Ideal if you're touring the inland sierras; this quintessentially Spanish hotel has rather small rooms of great charm.

✉ Carretera Pliego s/n
☎ 968 66 21 05

San Pedro del Pinatar
Balneario La Encarnación (€)
A charming old-world spa hotel surrounded by flowers, where you can bathe in the mineral-rich waters. Pretty tiled rooms and a warm welcome. (Open summer.)

✉ Condesa 2, Los Alcázares
☎ 968 57 50 04

Traina (€)
Situated between the Mar Menor and the Mediterranean, this is a relaxing base for exploring the coast and adjacent salt flats. Has rooms for the disabled.

✉ Av Generalísimo 84, Lo Pagán ☎ 968 33 50 22; www.hoteltraina.com

Spas
Murcia is well endowed with natural hot springs, whose waters relieve the discomfort of everything from arthritis to eczema. Most of them were used by the Romans and the Moors and they are still very popular. Spa hotels range from the incredibly luxurious, with beauty farms attached, to those emphasising treatments. Often in out-of-the-way places, they can make a peaceful base for exploring the inland areas, with the added bonus of a hot thermal swimming pool to ease away your aches and pains. (See Fortuna, ► 86).

Shopping in the Costa Blanca

Shops in Costa Blanca

The main resorts are crammed with shops and if you have forgotten something vital you should have no trouble in tracking it down – or in adding to your holiday wardrobe. Many coastal resorts also have a good selection of household and interior-design shops where you may find attractive ornaments, china and glass. Leather goods are usually a good buy, with soft and well-designed shoes top of the list. For serious shopping, the main towns of Alicante and Murcia have a good range of shops of all sorts; Gandía also prides itself on its facilities, with several shopping areas and markets for food and crafts.

Arts, Crafts & Gifts

Alfarería Bellón

A specialist ceramicist, making modern pots using shapes, techniques and colours reminiscent of the earliest Iberian ware.

✉ **Paseo Ollería 19, Totana**
☎ **968 42 48 01**

Artesanía

An interesting shop carrying a large, attractive range of ceramics, pottery and other crafts from the Alicante region.

✉ **V Pascual Alfonso X el Sabio 15, Alicante (Alacant)**
☎ **965 14 01 39**

Artesanía Abellán

A wonderful shop specialising in handmade Belén figures, the traditional miniatures used in Christmas cribs. The tiny figures represent not only the Virgin, Child, shepherds and kings, but a host of everyday people with their tools and implements.

✉ **Mayor 16, Bo del Progreso, Murcia** ☎ **968 25 28 06**

Centro Regional de Artesanía

Half-shop, half-exhibition, with the whole range of traditional Murcian handicrafts from all over the region, and information on where you can find the actual craftsmen.

✉ **Francisco Rabal 8, Murcia**
☎ **968 28 45 85** 🕐 **Mon–Fri 11–2, 4:30–7:30, Sat 11–2**

Cerámica les Sorts

Colourful pottery from all over Valencia is piled high in this crammed shop – everything from practical plates, bowls and jugs to mounds of ceramic fruit and dwarfs and gnomes.

✉ **Edif Kristal Mar 18D–18E, Moraira** ☎ **965 74 57 37**

Cerámicas Valles

You could spend hours pottering around this big showroom, which sells vibrant, hand-painted ceramics and pottery from all over Spain, as well as leather, garden pots and rather dubious paintings.

✉ **Urb. Los Piños D-5, Ctra Calpe-Moraira Km 2, Calpe**
☎ **965 833 661**

El Poveo

A well-known outlet for one of Totana's major ceramic producers, with pots and other products beautifully made in interesting shapes and colours.

✉ **Rambla s/n, Totana**
☎ **968 42 19 52**

Floristería Iris

A lovely flower shop which will deliver flowers and offers an overseas service.

✉ **Tomás Ortuño 82, Benidorm**
☎ **966 80 80 08**

La Tacita de Plata

If you are one of the many collectors of Lladró porcelain figures, this shop has an enormous range and all the new models.

✉ **Plaza Mayor 7/8, Benidorm**
☎ **966 58 27 69**

Mercadillo de Verano

A daily summer market with a fascinating mix of stalls selling traditional and modern crafts.

✉ **Esplanada de Cervantes, Dénia** ☎ **None**

Silk

An Aladdin's cave of gifts with a difference, that

specialises in hand-made crafts and textiles from India, China and Nepal.

✉ **C/ Médico Pascual Pérez 13, Alicante** ☎ **965 20 85 91**

Yelmo Antigüedades
One of the best antique shops in the Costa Blanca region but the prices are a bit on the high side.

✉ **Sagasta 34 and 42, Cartagena** ☎ **968 52 54 13**

Books & Stationery

Boutique de la Prensa
A good newspaper and magazine outlet with a large range of papers and periodicals from all over Europe.

✉ **Passeig de la Carretera 4, Benidorm** ☎ **965 85 03 07**

Ex Libris
This well-stocked bookstore has lovely photographic and art books, as well as an excellent selection of locally themed guide and picture books and maps. They also carry both Spanish and foreign magazines.

✉ **Plaza Jorge Juan 7, Dénia** ☎ **966 43 15 52**

Librería Internacional
An excellent and wide-ranging bookshop, with helpful staff, specialising in maps and charts.

✉ **Rafael Altamira 6, Alicante** ☎ **965 21 79 25**

Libros Escudero
Second-hand bookshop with a huge selection of English paperbacks, as well as old postcards, posters and cigarette cards.

✉ **Santa Faz 47, Benidorm** ☎ **650 57 55 20**

Fashion, Leather & Jewellery

Amor Amor
Clothes shop for women with a wide range of designs for many occasions.

✉ **Avenida Martínez Alejos 3, Benidorm** ☎ **965 85 13 95**

Bernardino
Wide selection of men's and women's shoes from this Elche-based manufacturer.

✉ **San Miguel 16** ☎ **965 45 21 93 and Diagonal 5, Elche (Elx)** ☎ **965 43 63 89**

Bolsos Paco
Deliciously soft bags, travel goods, belts, wallets and purses are sold here.

✉ **Patricio Ferrandiz 27, Dénia** ☎ **966 42 13 12**

Boutique Bolé Bolé
A ladies' clothes shop with a good range of classic and not-so-classic designs.

✉ **Plaza Ruperto Chapí 6, Alicante** ☎ **965 14 30 33**

Goya Oro
Upmarket jeweller selling top-name watches and elegant jewellery in platinum, gold and silver.

✉ **Martínez Alejos 3, Benidorm** ☎ **966 83 10 50**

Jacadi
This stylish shop has a good range of children's clothes for kids up to the age of 14.

✉ **Teatro 46, Alicante** ☎ **965 14 35 45**

Joyería Gómez
An upmarket jeweller with some attractive and typically Spanish designs. Good range of international watches.

✉ **Corredora 6, Elche** ☎ **965 45 28 50**

Centros Commerciales and Department Stores
Most visitors to Spain enjoy shopping in the vast hypermarkets that have sprung up since the 1970s for a huge range of food, drink, hardware and clothes. *Continente* is one of the best chains, with branches at Alicante, Benidorm, Elche, Oliva and Murcia.

The nationwide chain of *El Corte Inglés*, founded in 1939 to sell English fabrics, has good general department stores. There are branches at Alicante and Murcia.

Markets

There are two distinct main types of market in Spain; the *mercado municipal*, a daily food market, and the *mercadillos*, weekly street markets. Food markets are held in the heart of town, and have stalls selling fruit and vegetables, meat, fish, dairy products, bread and pastries and flowers. They are colourful and fascinating, the prices are controlled, and they are good places to put together a picnic. Street markets, on a specific day each week in all sizeable towns, are mostly devoted to clothes, shoes and household goods. They are fun to wander round and you can often pick up a bargain, but don't expect high style or quality. Tourist offices have details of their opening times and also of the huge Sunday-morning *mercadillos artesanos*, craft markets, held in various towns.

Marisol Moda

Shop entirely devoted to women's shirts and blouses – best buys include hand-embroidered pure cotton blouses and cheap-and-cheerful tops in bright colours. (Two branches.)

✉ **Paseo de la Carretera 10 and 44, Benidorm**
☎ **966 81 74 48**

Montesinos

An elegant outlet for fashions from one of Valencia's most prestigious designers.

✉ **Conde de Altea 18, Altea**
☎ **965 84 28 33**

Ritual

Pure cotton and silk skirts, trousers, shirts and dresses from India and the Far East, shawls and wraps, are piled high in this pretty shop. Perfect hot-weather wear.

✉ **Marques de Campo 26, Dénia** ☎ **966 43 01 19**

Salvador Artesano

Out-of-town factory outlet for one of Elche's main shoe and leather manufacturers. Search through for some amazing bargains.

✉ **Carretera Murcia–Alicante Km 45, Elche (Elx)**
☎ **966 67 54 41**

Saqueta

Soft leather bags, purses and wallets.

✉ **Mayor 17, Gandía**
☎ **962 87 97 92**

Stefano Orso

This well-stocked shop carries a good range of bags, purses, belts and other leather goods to cater for all tastes

✉ **Calle Gambo 4, Benidorm**
☎ **965 85 35 68**

Pecas Calzados

Two branches of a popular shoe shop with a wide range of styles at very good prices.

✉ **La Cruz 6** ☎ **962 87 73 16 and Mayor 60, Gandía**
☎ **962 87 69 44**

Perfumería Bernabeu

These sister stores carry a large range of makes and types of skin-care products and scents.

✉ **Mayor 42, Gandía** ☎ **962 87 65 40 and San Francisco de Borja 52** ☎ **962 87 42 11**

Volantins

A children's clothes shop for all ages from babies to sub-teens, ideal as gifts for the grandchildren.

✉ **Alfonso XIII 4, Gandía**
☎ **962 87 31 05**

Yacaré

This exquisite leather shop is one of Benidorm's few truly elegant stores. Classic bags, belts, purses and understated leather clothes.

✉ **Avda Mediterráneo 14, Benidorm** ☎ **966 80 54 06**

Food & Drink

Bodega Co-operativa San Isidro

Jumilla *denominación de origen* wines.

✉ **Carretera Murcia 32, Jumilla** ☎ **968 78 07 00**

Bodegas Fernández

And yet another wineshop selling Jumilla *denominación de origen* wines.

✉ **Avenida Murcia Km 37, Jumilla** ☎ **968 78 24 00**

Bodega Selección

An attractive wineshop that is well-stocked with over 400 different Spanish wines, *cavas* and liqueurs. There is also a selection of imported specialities.

✉ **Avenida Constitución 22A, Orihuela** ☎ 965 81 37 81

La Boutique del Vino
A wide range of Spanish and foreign wines, spirits and liqueurs – a good place to find that special bottle to take home.

✉ **Avda Ametlla de Mar s/n, Benidorm** ☎ 966 80 32 09

Convento de la Trinidad
Spanish nuns maintain the old tradition of cake, sweet and pastry making, using local recipes and the finest ingredients. Traditonal delicacies from Orihuela; give your order and the goodies will appear on a turn-table.

✉ **Convento de la Trinidad, C/ Overia 1, Orihuela** ☎ **No phone (enclosed order)**

Cooperativa Agrícola
Olive-oil enthusiasts can buy the best of the local oils straight from source here – sizes range from ½ litre bottles to 5-litre cans.

✉ **Mossén Eugeni Raduan 6, Cocentaina** ☎ 965 59 02 67

Damas
A wonderful bar and *pastelería*, with an huge range of sweet and savoury creations.

✉ **Pintor Lorenzo Casanova 5, Alicante** ☎ 965 12 14 71

Enacoteca Bernadino
A huge range (over 2,500) of Spanish vintages on offer in this upmarket wine merchant – they specialise in Rioja.

✉ **C/ Alberola 38, Alicante** ☎ 965 28 08 73

Especialities Lloret
This upmarket food shop is a real boon for self-caterers. Also a good range of tempting edible souvenirs.

✉ **Juan Carlos I-3, Villajoyosa (La Vila Joiosa)** ☎ 965 89 03 93

El Túnel
A good place to track down the traditional pastries and sweetmeats of Alcoy.

✉ **San Lorenzo 34, Alcoy (Alcoi)** ☎ 965 54 52 54

Fonda Negra
Old-established shop with a large range of high-quality Murcian foodstuffs.

✉ **González Adalid 1, Murcia** ☎ 968 21 15 63

L'Alteana
Sumptuous calorie-heavy bread and cakes as well as an interesting range of savoury mouthfuls.

✉ **Avenida de la Nucia 13, Altea** ☎ 965 84 03 07

Pasteleria Carlos
A mecca for the sweet-toothed with cakes, pastries and traditional sweetmeats that are beautiful to look at and delicious to eat.

✉ **Jaime el Conquistador 7, Murcia** ☎ 968 23 30 20

Pralines Soen
A mecca for chocaholics with a wide range of Spanish and Belgian chocolates.

✉ **Calle Gambo 2** ☎ **966 80 73 94 and Avenida Gabriel Miró 41, Calpe (Calp)** ☎ 965 83 59 59

Sanct Bernhard
An interesting herbalist, worth visiting for its wide range of products including teas, creams and cleansers.

✉ **Avenida Gabriel Miró 7, Calpe (Calp)** ☎ 965 83 68 07

Centros de Artesanía
Murcia is justly proud of the range and quality of hand-produced crafts made within its borders, which range from pottery and woodwork to fabrics and embroidery. The regional government has set up centres in several major towns specifically to help the artisans involved by showing and selling their work under one roof. Here, interested visitors can see the full range of Murcian crafts, buy anything that appeals to them, or be advised on where to find something specific. These centres are well worth a visit and you can find them in Murcia, Cartagena and Lorca.

Children's Activities

Take Care
Do remember that Spanish summer sun is hot and strong and make certain your children are well protected, keeping them in the shade during the middle of the day when the sun is hottest. Use plenty of high-factor sun-cream and persuade them to wear hats and cover up for the first few days; better a wet T-shirt than a miserable sun-burnt child.

Alicante & Around

Alicante (Alacant)
Costa Blanca Express
All children will enjoy a ride on this narrow-gauge train which ambles up the coast from Alicante to Dénia, stopping en route. Go all the way with older kids or one or two stops only with the little ones, have a swim and some lunch and come home later in the day.
✉ Alicante ☎ 965 26 27 31, Benidorm ☎ 965 85 18 95, and Dénia ☎ 965 78 04 45
🕐 6AM–9PM

Torrevieja
Aquapolis
A big aquapark with pools, hydrotubs and plenty of slides and rides for the children, with water mountains and artificial waves. Nicely laid out with restaurants and a picnic area.
✉ Finca la Olla Grande s/n
☎ 965 71 58 90 🕐 Mid-Jun to mid-Sep 11–7

Benidorm & the North

Benidorm
Aqualandia Verano
The biggest, best-known and most popular aquapark in Benidorm. A wide selection of rides, slides and pools.
✉ Sierra Helada, Partida Bayo
☎ 965 86 01 00 🕐 Jun–Sep 11–7 🚌 2, 7

Barco a la Isla
Enjoy a boat trip out to Benidorm Island, a nature reserve just off the coast, especially in a glass-bottomed boat.
✉ Puerto de Benidorm ☎ 965 85 00 52 🕐 Hourly from 11–7

Festilandia
A good amusement park for very small children right in the heart of Benidorm.
✉ Avenida del Mediterráneo 20
☎ 965 85 41 26 🕐 11–7

Karting la Cala
A chance for older children to test their skill and nerves on one of Europe's largest go-karting tracks.
✉ Avenida Villaiosa 11
☎ 965 89 46 76 🕐 Winter 11–7; summer 11–8

Mundomar
A marine park with a dolphin show, but seals and parrots are popular too and there's a maze of wooded, rocky paths and water features to explore.
✉ Sierra Helada, Rincón de Loix ☎ 965 86 91 01 🕐 10–6 🚌 2, 7

Museo de Cera
Over a 100 wax figures of famous Spanish and international personalities, intriguing most children, who will recognise many of them.
✉ Avenida Mediterráneo 8
☎ 966 80 84 21 🕐 10–7 🚌 2

Terra Mítica
A spectacularly large, new 'World of Myth' theme park which opened in summer 2000 near Benidorm. Visitors can enjoy rides, shows and theatre events in five areas based on past Mediterranean civilisations – Egypt, Greece, Rome, Iberia and the Islands. Among the rides are a log flume and the largest wooden rollercoaster in Europe (the second largest in the world). Some of the major rides are replicated in miniature for smaller children. Each area has themed shops,

restaurants and bars.

📧 Ctra Benidorm a Finestrat,
Camino del Moralet s/n
☎ 966 83 51 86 🕐 Summer,
10AM–midnight; mid Sep–Oct,
10–8; winter 10–6

Calpe (Calp)
Aquascope
A semi-submersible boat with
an underwater glass
observation chamber which
makes trips around the Peñón
de Ifach, giving non-scuba-
divers and children a chance
to see the wide variety of sea
life without getting wet.

📧 Puerto de Calpe
☎ 965 83 85 32
🕐 Summer only, hourly from 11

Guadalest
Museo del Juguete
Antiguo 1790–1959
A toy museum with an
enormous collection from all
over the world; most parents
will get nostalgic over the
comic collection and there's
a reproduction of a 1929
school classroom.

📧 Guadalest ☎ 965 88 52 66
🕐 10–7 🚌 From Benidorm

Játiva (Xàtiva)
El Castell
The ultimate in castles,
complete with towers, look-
out points, cannons and
walkways, will appeal to
many children, as will a drink
at the panoramic bar.

📧 Carretera Castillo ☎ 962
27 33 46 🕐 Winter 10–6;
summer 10–7 🚌 Tourist train at
12 and 4 from outside tourist
office at Alameda de Jaume I 50

Penaguila
Safari Aitana
A safari park in the Aitana
Sierra behind the coast with
the usual collections of lions,
giraffes, elephants and other

animals. 't's a good choice in
hot weather, when you can
have a swim in the pool.

📧 Carretera Villajoyosa (La
Vila Joiosa)–Benidorm
☎ 965 52 92 73 🕐 11–7

Vergel (Verger)
Safari Park Vergel
A drive-round safari park near
the beaches; a chance to see
a dolphin show.

📧 Carretera Vergel–Pego
☎ 965 75 02 85 🕐 11–7

Murcia

Cartagena
Museo Nacional de
Arqueología Marítima
Collection of treasures from
the sea-bed. Exhibits include
piles of amphora, used for
transporting goods in ancient
times, and a reconstruction
of a perfectly loaded ship.

📧 Dique de Navidad s/n,
Puerto de Cartagena
☎ 968 10 11 66 🕐 Tue–Sun
10–3. Closed Mon

La Manga
Excursiones Joven Maria
Dolores
Daily boat trips out to the
islands in the Mar Menor
which children will enjoy as a
change from the beach.

📧 From Santiago de la Ribera
and Los Alcázares ☎ 629 60 71
47 🕐 15 Jun–30 Sep. Groups in
winter by appointment only

Murcia
Museo de la Ciencia
A good science museum,
with water as its main
theme. Many hands-on
exhibits and a children's
planetarium.

📧 Plaza de la Ciencia 1
☎ 968 21 19 98 🕐 Tue–Fri
10–1, 4–8; Sat 10–2, 5–8; Sun
11–2 🚌 7a

Children Welcome
Spaniards love children
and make them welcome
everywhere; local kids stay
up late so there is no need
to leave yours at home in
the evenings, they will be
welcome at all but the
grandest restaurants.
Encourage them to say
hola (hello) and *gracias*
(thank you), two words
which go a long way to
winning local hearts.

Cinema, Theatre & Concerts

Nightlife
Unsurprisingly, the Costa Blanca has an animated night scene, the streets busy until the early hours of the morning. Benidorm has numerous discos and clubs and an eclectic range of music. The club to be seen at varies from year to year and word of mouth should lead you in the right direction. Many popular clubs are situated in huge buildings outside towns, usually just a taxi hop away. Many bars have live music with jazz, easy listening and even the occasional burst of flamenco on offer. The larger hotels often have after-dinner dancing. Opening times are flexible, but the action starts very late, often after midnight, and carries on till around dawn. Prices vary, with some clubs charging a hefty entrance fee, which usually includes one free drink.

Despite the large number of foreign residents in the area there is little foreign-language entertainment on the Costa Blanca. Benidorm has a number of venues with floor shows and cabarets which need no translation, and cinemas in the main resorts occasionally feature foreign-language films. Alicante and Murcia both have a lively Spanish arts scene, with theatre, classical concerts and occasional ballet and opera; you can get details from the tourist offices.

Weekly newspapers are published in English, German and Dutch on the coast; these carry details of what's on where.

Alicante (Alacant)
Teatro Principal
✉ Plaza Ruperto Chapí 7
☎ 965 21 91 57

Altea
Palau Altea
Altea's millenium arts centre has a full programme of music, theatre and dance.
✉ Palau Altea, Casc Antic
☎ 966 88 19 24

Elche (Elx)
Gran Teatro
Mixed programme of theatre, classical music and films in Spanish.
✉ Hospital 26
☎ 965 45 14 03

Orihuela
Teatro Circo
Wide range of concerts, theatre and shows for Spanish-speakers, housed in a beautifully restored turn-of-the-century circular theatre.
✉ Ronda de Santo Domingo

Benidorm
Benidorm Palace
Very popular international floorshow and cabaret with optional dinner.
✉ Avenida Dr Severo Ochoa s/n ☎ 965 85 16 60

Castillo Fortaleza de Alfaz
The castle offers a night out at a mock medieval banquet followed by a visit to a chamber of horrors and a futuristic disco.
✉ Carretera Benidorm–Albir
☎ 966 86 55 92

El Centro Cinema
✉ Murcia s/n
☎ 965 85 83 12

Molino Benidorm
Amusing floorshow followed by male striptease.
✉ Avenida Beniardá 2
☎ 966 80 23 08

Sabrina
Another saucy show including male striptease.
✉ Avenida Jaime 1
☎ 965 85 36 06

Calpe (Calp)
Alhambra Cinema
English-language films shown on Wednesdays.
✉ Conde de Altea 7
☎ 965 83 03 84

Gata de Gorgos
Europa Cinema
English-language films shown on Tuesdays.
✉ Escolar 14 ☎ (965) 75 62 62

Murcia
Teatro Romea
Full programme of Spanish theatre and music in the handsome 19th-century theatre.
✉ Plaza Julián Romea 7
☎ 968 21 16 11

Casinos, Bars & Nightclubs

Casinos

Casinos in the Costa Blanca generally offer roulette, *chemin de fer* and blackjack and some have slot machines and private gaming rooms. Dress is normally casual-smart. You must be over 18 to enter. Remember to take your passport as well.

Alicante
Casino de Alicante
🖂 Explanada de España 16
☎ 965 20 56 11 🕐 9PM–4AM

Villajoyosa (La Vila Joiosa)
Casino Costa Blanca
🖂 Carretera Alicante–Valencia Km 141.5 ☎ 965 89 07 00
🕐 9PM–4AM

Cartagena
Casino Cartagena
🖂 Mayor 17 ☎ 968 50 10 10
🕐 10–2, 5–11

Murcia
Gran Casino Murcia
🖂 Apostoles 34 ☎ 968 21 23 08
🕐 6PM–4AM

La Manga
Casino del Mar Menor
🖂 Gran Via La Manga s/n
☎ 968 14 06 04 🕐 Sun–Thu 9PM–4AM, Fri, Sat 9PM–5AM

Bars & Nightclubs

Alicante
Pachá
Lively disco on one of the town's main streets with a clientele of all ages.
🖂 Avenida de Aguilera 38
☎ None 🕐 11PM–6AM

Benidorm
KM
KM has a long-standing reputation for its music, terraces and beautiful people.
🖂 Antigua Ctra N-332 ☎ None
🕐 11PM–6AM, Easter–Oct

Penélope
This huge, noisy and sophisticated disco has been popular with Benidorm regulars for years.
🖂 Antigua Ctra N-322 ☎ None
🕐 11PM–6AM

Dénia
Imperial
Just outside town on the main Jávea road, this action-packed disco has terraced bars and features the latest music and dance.
🖂 Carretera Jávea ☎ None
🕐 10:30PM–5AM, Easter–Oct

La Manga
Zeppelin
One of the liveliest disco bars along La Manga's main boulevard, with the action starting late and continuing often until after dawn.
🖂 Gran Via de la Manga
☎ None 🕐 11PM–6AM

Murcia
Discoteca The Night Club
Really starts to hum after 1AM when most people arrive.
🖂 Puerta Nueva ☎ None
🕐 11:30PM–6AM, Thu–Sat

Santa Pola
Discoteca Camelot
People drive miles to this incredibly popular disco which features all the latest music and dance crazes.
🖂 Gran Playa ☎ None
🕐 11PM–6AM

Bullfighting

Whatever your feelings about the ethics of this essentially Spanish experience, bullfighting is a fact of life here and every town of any size has a bullring. Fights take place on Sunday afternoons throughout the summer season and there are large rings in Alicante, Benidorm and Murcia as well as some of the smaller towns.

Sport

Golf

The Costa Blanca area has over 20 prestigious and beautifully laid-out golf courses, as well as some smaller ones, and the game brings many visitors to the area. Golf package holidays are increasingly popular. Most courses have clubs and trolleys or buggies for hire and a full range of ancillary services, such as practice ranges, pro shops and club houses. You may be asked for a handicap certificate and you should book in advance as courses can be very busy.

Sport

The main emphasis is on outdoor and water-based sports. Sailing and scuba-diving are the most popular, with excellent facilities in the major resorts, while golf courses have multiplied. Cyclists and walkers will find great opportunities in the hills behind the coast. Most places have tennis courts and larger centres offer a good programme of spectator sports, from football and rugby to athletics.

Bowling

Benidorm
Bowling Centre Benidorm
✉ Avenida Mediterráneo 22
☎ 965 85 41 87

Bowling Green Benidorm
✉ Partida Almafrá s/n
☎ 965 85 77 43

Golf

Alicante (Alacant)
Club de Golf Alenda
✉ Autovía Alicante–Madrid Km 15 ☎ 965 62 05 21

Calpe (Calp)
Club de Golf Don Cayo
✉ Urbanización El Aramo–Sierra de Altea
☎ 965 84 80 46

Dénia
Club de Golf La Sella
✉ Carretera La Xara–Jesús Pobre ☎ 966 45 42 52

Jávea (Xàbia)
Club de Golf Jávea
✉ Carretera Jávea–Benita-chell Km 4.5 ☎ 965 79 25 84

La Manga
Club de Golf Los Belones
✉ La Manga Club Hyatt

Complex ☎ 968 13 72 34

Club de Golf Torre Pacheco
✉ Torre Pacheco
☎ 968 57 90 37

Moraira
Club de Golf Ifach
✉ Carretera Moraira–Calpe Km 3, Urbanización San Jaime
☎ 966 49 71 14

Orihuela
Club de Golf Villa Martín
✉ Carretera Alicante–Cartagena Km 50
☎ 966 76 51 27

Riding

Alicante (Alacant)
Club Hípico de Campoamor
✉ Carretera Cartagena–Alicante Km 48
☎ 965 32 13 66

Dénia
Escuela de Equitación La Sella
✉ Carretera La Xara–Jesús Pobre ☎ 965 76 14 55

La Manga
El Puntal
✉ La Manga Club Hyatt Complex, Los Belones
☎ 968 13 73 05

Peque Park
✉ La Manga del Mar Menor
☎ 968 13 72 39

Sailing

Alicante (Alacant)
Club Náutico Costa Blanca
✉ Avenida de la Condomina 20
☎ 965 15 44 91

Águilas
Club Náutico Islas Menores
✉ Puerto Marítima, Cartagena
☎ 968 13 33 55

Dénia
Club Náutico Dénia
✉ Carretera Dénia–Jávea 1
☎ 965 78 09 89

La Manga
Surf-Playa
✉ La Manga del Mar Menor
☎ 968 14 00 20

Mazarrón
Club Náutico de Mazarrón
✉ Cabezo de Cebada s/n
☎ 968 59 40 11

Moraira
Antipodes Sailing School
✉ Puerto de Moraira
☎ 965 83 83 10

Santa Pola
Club Náutico de Santa Pola
✉ Muella de Poniente s/n
☎ 965 41 24 03

Scuba Diving
There are several stretches of protected coastline along the Costa Blanca with a rich underwater marine life. You can dive under supervision with the many diving clubs; if you want to dive alone bring your international proficiency certificate.

Benidorm
Costa Blanca Sub
✉ Santander 20, Edif Coblanca
XX ☎ 966 80 17 84

Club Poseidon
✉ Santander 9, Alfaz 4, Edif Silvia ☎ 965 85 32 27

Águilas
La Almadraba
✉ Ernest Hemingway 13, Calabardina ☎ 968 41 96 32

Cabo de Palos
Islas Hormigas Club
✉ Cabo de Palos
☎ 968 14 55 30

Calpe (Calp)
Peñón Divers-Buceo
✉ Aquagym Esmeralda, Ponent
1 ☎ 966 83 61 01

Cartagena
Nereidas Diving
✉ Puerto de Cartagena
☎ 968 31 39 87

Dénia
Aquatic Dénia
✉ Carretera Dénia–Jávea 3d, Les Rotes ☎ 966 42 52 15

Mazarrón
Zoea Mazarrón
✉ Plaza del Mar 20
☎ 968 15 40 06

Swimming
Beaches in Costa Blanca, (▶ 82–3) which vary up and down the coast from shingle and pebbles to the finest sand, often sport the Blue Flag award, which guarantees their cleanliness, safety and facilities. The main towns – Alicante, Benidorm and Murcia – all have covered heated indoor pools for winter swimming.

Waterskiing

Benidorm
Cable Ski
✉ Racó de l'Oix, Playa de Levante ☎ 965 85 13 86

Windsurfing

Calpe (Calp)
Escuela de Windsurf Waikiki
✉ Playa de Levante
☎ 965 83 28 56

La Manga
Multisports Centre Mar Menor
✉ La Manga del Mar Menor
☎ 968 57 00 21

Watersports
With its mild winter and long hot summers the coast provides ideal conditions for watersports practically year-round. Marina facilities are excellent everywhere. Inexperienced mariners will find sailing schools at all the main resorts with hire and tuition available; the sheltered Mar Menor being a particularly good spot for beginners. Windsurfing and waterskiing are also on offer and the warm shallow waters of the Mar Menor are a real draw. There are plenty of boat excursions up and down the Costa Blanca.

115

What's On When

Moros y Cristianos

Forty-six provincial towns in Alicante (Alacant) hold Moros y Cristianos festivals to celebrate the Reconquest; they take the form of often lavishly costumed historical re-enactments of key events during the years leading to the Moors' expulsion, with processions, fireworks, music, and traditional food and drink. Not tourist events, they help give a superb insight into the soul of the region.

January

Los Reyes Magos: parades to celebrate the arrival of the Three Kings, in towns all over the Costa Blanca.
Porrate de San Antón (Fira i Porrat de Sant Antoni): a countryside festival with parades, decorated traditional horse-drawn carts, a food festival and a blessing of farm animals, Alicante, Benidorm.

February

Carnaval: a pre-Lent carnival with parades and dancing in fancy dress, takes place in many towns.

March/April

Semana Santa: week-long deeply religious Holy Week celebrations in towns everywhere and particularly noteworthy in Cartagena, Jumilla, Murcia, Moratalla, Mula, Orihuela, Alicante and Elche (Elx).
Peregrina de Santa Faz: 100,000-strong pilgrimage to the monastery at Santa Faz, Alicante.
Fiesta de la Primavera: parades and fireworks in the week following Holy Week; it includes the *Bando de la Huerta* (Orchard Procession) and the *Entierra de la Sardina* (Burial of the Sardine), Murcia.
Fallas de San José: fire-festival with effigies burnt on pyres, Dénia.
Moros y Cristianos: the most important of the numerous festivals held to celebrate the Reconquest, Alcoy (Alcoi).
Semana Mediterránea de la Música: with top classical performers and orchestras from around the world, Alicante.

June

Hogueras de San Juan: week-long midsummer festival with parades, fireworks and bullfights, Alicante. Smaller *hogueras* in Dénia, Calpe (Calp), Benidorm and Jávea (Xàbia).

July

Festival Español de la Canción: major Spanish song festival, Benidorm.
Moros y Cristianos: spectacular historical mock-battle on beach, Villajoyosa (La Vila Joiosa).
Fiesta de la Virgen del Carmen: processions, boat races, fireworks, Villajoyosa, Tabarca, San Pedro.

August

Festival de las Habaneras: festival of Cuban song-form brought back by salt-exporters, Torrevieja.
Misteri d'Elx, La Festa: superb medieval mystery play in two parts, celebrating the Assumption of the Virgin, Elche.
Moros y Cristianos: historical festival with the protagonists arriving from the sea, Dénia and Jávea.
Fiesta de la Vendimia: the town fountain runs with wine to celebrate the start of the wine harvest, Jumilla.
Festival Nacional del Canta de las Minas: one of the Spain's most important flamenco events, La Unión.

September

Festival de Folklore del Mediterráneo: international festival, Murcia.

October, November and December

Small local festivals, listed under town entries.

Practical Matters

Above: *refreshment time at one of the off-street cafes*
Right: *holiday-makers under tuition at one of the region's many sailing schools*

117

TIME DIFFERENCES

GMT
12 noon

→
Spain
1PM

→
Germany
1PM

←
USA (NY)
7AM

→
Netherlands
1PM

→
France
1PM

BEFORE YOU GO

WHAT YOU NEED

		UK	Germany	USA	Netherlands
● Required ○ Suggested ▲ Not required	Some countries require a passport to remain valid for a minimum period (usually at least six months) beyond the date of entry – contact their consulate or embassy or your travel agent for details.				
Passport/national identity card		●	●	●	●
Visa		▲	▲	▲	▲
Onward or return ticket		▲	▲	●	▲
Health inoculations		▲	▲	▲	▲
Health documentation (Health, ➤ 123),		●	●	●	●
Travel insurance		○	○	○	○
Driving licence (national with Spanish translation or international)		●	●	●	●
Car insurance certificate		●	●	●	●
Car registration document		●	●	●	●

WHEN TO GO

Costa Blanca

High season

Low season

14°C	15°C	17°C	18°C	22°C	26°C	29°C	29°C	28°C	23°C	18°C	15°C
JAN	FEB	MAR	APR	MAY	JUN	JUL	AUG	SEP	OCT	NOV	DEC

Wet   Cloud   Sun   Sunshine and showers

TOURIST OFFICES

In the UK
Spanish Tourist Office
22–23 Manchester Square
London W1M 5AP
☎ 020 7486 8077
fax: 020 7486 8034

In the USA
Tourist Office of Spain
666 5th Avenue
New York
NY 10103
☎ 212/265 8822
fax: 212/265 8864

POLICE (Policía Nacional) 091 FIRE (Bomberos) 085

AMBULANCE (Ambulància) Alicante 965 11 46 76

RED CROSS (Cruz Roja) Alicante 965 25 25 25, Benidorm

965 85 30 42, Murcia 968 22 22 22

WHEN YOU ARE THERE

ARRIVING

Spain's national airline, Iberia (☎ 0990 341 341:
www.iberia.com) has scheduled flights to Alicante's
El Altet and Valencia's Manises airports from major
Spanish and European cities.

El Altet Airport
Kilometres to city centre

Journey times

 N/A

40 minutes

15 minutes

10 kilometres

Manises Airport
Kilometres to city centre

Journey times

N/A

45 minutes

20 minutes

15 kilometres

MONEY

Spain's currency is the euro which is divided into 100
cents. Coins come in denominations of 1, 2, 5, 10, 20
and 50 cents, 1 and 2 euros, and notes come in 5, 10,
20, 50, 100, 200 and 500 euro denominations (the last
two are rarely seen). The notes and one side of the
coins are the same throughout the European single
currency zone. Notes and coins from any of the other
countries can be used in Spain.

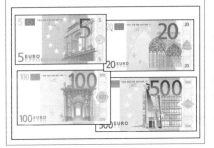

TIME

 Like the rest of
Spain, the Costa
Blanca is one hour
ahead of Greenwich Mean
Time (GMT+1), but from late
March until late October
summer time (GMT+2)
operates.

CUSTOMS

YES
From another EU
country for
personal use (guidelines)
800 cigarettes, 200 cigars,
1 kilogram of tobacco
10 litres of spirits (over 22%)
20 litres of aperitifs
90 litres of wine, of which 60
litres can be sparkling wine
110 litres of beer

From a non-EU country for
your personal use, the
allowances are:
200 cigarettes OR
50 cigars OR
250 grams of tobacco
1 litre of spirits (over 22%)
2 litres of intermediary
products (eg sherry) and
sparkling wine
2 litres of still wine
50 grams of perfume
0.25 litres of eau de toilette

The value limit for goods is
175 euros

Travellers under 17 years of
age are not entitled to the
tobacco and alcohol
allowances.

 NO
Drugs, firearms,
ammunition,
offensive weapons, obscene
material, unlicensed animals.

EMBASSIES AND CONSULATES

UK
965 21 60 22

Germany
965 21 70 60

USA
965 21 60 22

Netherlands
965 21 21 75

WHEN YOU ARE THERE

TOURIST OFFICES

Tourist Information Telephone Service
☎ 901 300 600

Tourist Information Offices

● **Alicante (Alacant)**
Rambla Méndez Núñez 23
Alicante 03002
☎ 965 20 00 00

● **Benidorm**
Avenida Martínez Alejos 6
Benidorm 03500
☎ 965 85 32 24/
965 85 13 11

● **Dénia**
Plaza Oculista Buigues 9
Dénia 03700
☎ 966 42 23 67

● **Elche (Elx)**
Parque Municipal
Paseo de la Estácion
Elche 03203
☎ 965 45 27 47

● **Murcia**
Plaza del Romea 4
☎ 902 10 10 70

● **Orihuela**
Palacio Rubalcava
Calle Franciso Diez 25
Orihuela 0330
☎ 965 30 27 47

Other offices include: Altea, Águilas, Benissa, Calpe (Calp), Cartagena, Gandía, Jávea (Xàbia), Mazarrón, Santa Pola, Torrevieja, Villajoyosa (La Vila Joiosa) and Játiva (Xàtiva).

NATIONAL HOLIDAYS

J	F	M	A	M	J	J	A	S	O	N	D
2		(1)	(1)	1			1		1	1	2

1 Jan	New Year's Day
6 Jan	Epiphany
Mar/Apr	Good Friday, Easter Monday
1 May	Labour Day
15 Aug	Assumption of the Virgin
12 Oct	National Day
1 Nov	All Saints' Day
6 Dec	Constitution Day
25 Dec	Christmas Day

Many shops and offices close for longer periods around Christmas and Easter, as well as for the festivals of Corpus Christi in May/June and the local holiday of the *comunidad valenciano* on 9 October.

OPENING HOURS

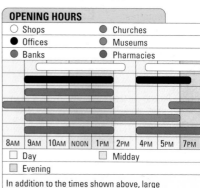

○ Shops	● Churches
● Offices	● Museums
● Banks	● Pharmacies

8AM	9AM	10AM	NOON	1PM	2PM	4PM	5PM	7PM

□ Day	□ Midday
□ Evening	

In addition to the times shown above, large department stores, as well as supermarkets and shops in tourist resorts, may open outside these times, especially in summer. In general, pharmacies, banks and shops close on Saturday afternoon, though banks may stay open until 4:30PM Monday to Thursday, October to May, but close Saturday, June to September. At least one chemist remains on duty in each town outside normal hours and at night. The opening times of museums is just a rough guide; some are open longer hours in summer than winter. Some museums close at weekends or another day in the week.

DRIVE ON THE
RIGHT

TOILETS
FREE

PUBLIC TRANSPORT

 Trains The Costa Blanca is served by two railway systems; one links the main towns and runs to Madrid; the other is a scenic narrow-gauge line along the coast from Alicante to Dénia. The main RENFE (the Spanish railway network) lines link Cartagena, Alicante and Valencia, Alicante and Madrid, and Cartagena with Murcia (☎ 965 92 02 02, bookings – English language, ☎ 902 24 02 02; www.renfe.es). The Costa Blanca Express, run by FEVE, leaves Alicante hourly from its own station and runs along the coast, stopping at virtually every station. Trains go as far as Benidorm, with about half completing the 2 hour 15 minute journey to Dénia (information and reservations: ☎ 966 80 31 03).

 Costa Blanca Buses Alicante's bus station (☎ 965 20 07 00) is located on the Calle Portugal, from where buses leave for all over the province and further afield. There are several different companies serving the area; their buses run hourly along the coast and link the province's towns. Tickets, with numbered seats, are bought in advance, and tourist information offices can provide details. In Murcia buses run from the bus station on Calle Sierra Nevada (☎ 968 29 22 11).

 Boat Trips Tabarca is the main island of the cluster lying off the coast to the south of Alicante; excursion ferries run from Alicante, Santa Pola and Torrevieja from April to November, giving a day on the island to explore and swim (information: Kontiki Alicante, ☎ 965 21 63 96; Barco Santa Pola a Tabarca, ☎ 965 41 11 13; Cruceros Tabardo ☎ 966 70 21 22).

 Urban Transport Local buses serve the main towns. Timetables and maps are available at local tourist information offices.

CAR RENTAL

 The leading international car rental companies have offices at Alicante airport and you can book a car in advance (essential in peak periods) either direct or through a travel agent. There are also car hire companies in most of the main towns and resorts.

TAXIS

 Hired at ranks (indicated by a blue square with a 'T'), on the street (by flagging down those with a green light/*libre* sign), or at hotels. They are good value, but may legally only carry four people. Check the approximate fare before setting out. A tariff list is displayed at taxi ranks.

DRIVING

 Speed limit on motorways (autopistas): **120kph**

 Speed limit on main roads: **100kph**

 Speed limit on minor roads: **90kph**

 Must be worn in front seats at all times and in rear seats where fitted.

 Limit: 80 micrograms of alcohol in 100ml of breath.

 Fuel (*gasolina*) is available in four grades: Super Plus (98 octane), Super (96 octane) and often unleaded (*sin plomo*), Mezcla or Normal (90 octane), and *gasoleo* or *gasoil* (diesel). Petrol stations are normally open 6AM–10PM, and closed Sundays, though larger ones (often self-service) are open 24 hours. Most take credit cards. There are few petrol stations in the remote inland areas and they may not carry the full range of fuels.

 If you break down driving your own car and are a member of an AIT-affiliated motoring club, you can call the Real Automóvil Club de España (☎ 915 93 33 33). If the car is hired, follow the instructions given in the documentation; most of the international rental firms provide a rescue service.

CENTIMETRES
INCHES

PERSONAL SAFETY

The national police force, the Policía Nacional (blue uniforms) keep law and order in urban areas. Some resorts have their own tourist-friendly Policía Turística. If you need a police station ask for *la comisaría*.

To help prevent crime:
- Do not carry more cash than you need
- Do not leave valuables on the beach or poolside
- Beware of pickpockets in markets, tourist sights or crowded places
- Avoid walking alone in dark alleys at night

Police assistance:
☎ **091**
from any call box

TELEPHONES

A public telephone (*teléfono*) takes all denomination euro coins. A phonecard (*credifone*) is available from tabacos and many supermarkets for €5 and €10. The code for Alicante province is 965 and for Murcia 968. To call the international operator dial 1005 (in Europe) or 025 (outside Europe). The number for Directory Enquiries is 1003.

International Dialling Codes	
From Spain to	
UK:	**00 44**
Germany:	**00 49**
USA & Canada:	**00 1**
Netherlands:	**00 31**

POST

Post offices (*correos*) are open 9AM–2PM but some also open in the afternoon and on Saturday morning. The main post office in Alicante at Plaza Gabriel Mirò is open Monday to Friday 8AM–9PM (2PM Saturday). Murcia's main office at Plaza de Ceballos is open Monday to Friday 9AM–2PM, 5–8PM (to 2PM Saturday). Stamps may also be bought in *tabacos*. Post boxes are yellow.

ELECTRICITY

The power supply on the Costa Blanca is: 220–225 volts.

Sockets accept two-round-pin-style plugs, so an adaptor is needed for most non-Continental appliances and a transformer for appliances operating on 110–120 volts.

TIPS/GRATUITIES

Yes ✓ No ✗		
Restaurants (if service not inc.)	✓	10%
Cafés/bar (if service not inc.)	✓	change
Tour guides	✓	€1–2
Hairdressers	✓	change
Taxis	✓	10%
Chambermaids/porters	✓	€1–2
Theatre/cinema usherettes	✓	change
Cloakrooms attendants	✓	change
Toilets	✗	

What to photograph: beaches, mountains, country villages, attractive harbours, markets, vineyards and olive and fruit groves.

When to photograph: the Spanish summer sun can be powerful at the height of the day, making photos taken at this time appear 'flat'; it is best to photograph in the early morning or late evening.

Where to buy film: film and camera batteries are readily available from tourist shops and *droguerías*.

HEALTH

Insurance
Nationals of EU and certain other countries can get medical treatment in Spain with the relevant documentation (Form E111 for Britons), although private medical insurance is still advised and is essential for all other visitors.

Dental Services
Dental treatment is not usually available free of charge as all dentists practise privately. A list of *dentistas* can be found in the yellow pages of the telephone directory. Dental treatment should be covered by private medical insurance.

Sun Advice
The sunniest (and hottest) months are July and August with an average of 11 hours sun a day and daytime temperatures of 32°C. Particularly during these months you should avoid the midday sun and use a strong sunblock.

Drugs
Prescription and non-prescription drugs and medicines are available from pharmacies (*farmacias*), distinguished by a large green cross. Spanish pharmacists are highly trained and can dispense many drugs that would be available only on prescription in other countries.

Safe Water
Tap water is generally safe though it can be heavily chlorinated. Mineral water is cheap to buy and is sold as *con gaz* (carbonated) and *sin gaz* (still). Drink plenty of water during hot weather.

CONCESSIONS

Students Holders of an International Student Identity Card can obtain some concessions on travel, entrance fees etc, but the major package-holiday resorts are not really geared up for students, being more suited for families and senior citizens. Package tours and camping offer excellent value and there are hostels and inexpensive hotels in the main towns for the more inquisitive traveller.

Senior Citizens The Costa Blanca is an excellent destination for older travellers, especially in winter when the resorts are quieter, prices more reasonable and hotels offer very economical long-stay rates. The best deals are available through tour operators who specialise in holidays for senior citizens.

CLOTHING SIZES

Costa Blanca	UK	Europe	USA	
46	36	46	36	Suits
48	38	48	38	Suits
50	40	50	40	Suits
52	42	52	42	Suits
54	44	54	44	Suits
56	46	56	46	Suits
41	7	41	8	Shoes
42	7.5	42	8.5	Shoes
43	8.5	43	9.5	Shoes
44	9.5	44	10.5	Shoes
45	10.5	45	11.5	Shoes
46	11	46	12	Shoes
37	14.5	37	14.5	Shirts
38	15	38	15	Shirts
39/40	15.5	39/40	15.5	Shirts
41	16	41	16	Shirts
42	16.5	42	16.5	Shirts
43	17	43	17	Shirts
34	8	34	6	Dresses
36	10	36	8	Dresses
38	12	38	10	Dresses
40	14	40	12	Dresses
42	16	42	14	Dresses
44	18	44	16	Dresses
38	4.5	38	6	Shoes
38	5	39	6.5	Shoes
39	5.5	39	7	Shoes
39	6	39	7.5	Shoes
40	6.5	40	8	Shoes
41	7	41	8.5	Shoes

WHEN DEPARTING

- Remember to contact the airport or your tour company representative on the day before leaving to ensure the flight details are unchanged.
- Spanish customs officials are usually polite and normally willing to negotiate.

LANGUAGE

The language that you hear on the streets in the towns and villages of Alicante is likely to be either Castilian (Spanish proper) or Valencian, a written and spoken language closely related to Catalan, which since 1982 has been on equal footing with Spanish in the region of Valencia. Valencian thrives in large pockets throughout Alicante province but Spanish is widely spoken, particularly in the major tourist centres. Street signs, maps and newspapers are not yet consistently bilingual and for the visitor, Spanish still dominates in those places where English is not spoken. Murcia has always been Spanish-speaking.

hotel	*hotel*	chambermaid	*camarera*
breakfast	*desayuno*	bath	*baño*
single room	*habitación indivual*	shower	*ducha*
		toilet	*lavabo*
double room	*habitación doble*	balcony	*balcón*
one person	*una persona*	key	*llave*
one night	*una noche*	lift	*ascensor*
reservation	*reservacíon*	sea view	*vista al mar*

bank	*banco*	travellers' cheque	*cheque de viajero*
exchange office	*oficina de cambio*	credit card	*tarjeta de crédito*
post office	*correos*		
coin	*moneda*	change money	*cambiar dinero*
money	*dinero*	cashier	*cajero*
cheque	*cheque*	foreign currency	*moneda extranjera*
bank card	*tarjeta del banco*		

café	*cafè*	starter	*primer plato*
pub/bar	*bar*	main course	*plato principal*
breakfast	*desayuno*	dessert	*postre*
lunch	*almuerzo*	bill	*cuenta*
dinner	*cena*	beer	*cerveza*
table	*mesa*	wine	*vino*
waiter	*camarero*	water	*agua*
waitress	*camarera*	coffee	*café*

aeroplane	*avión*	ticket	*billete*
airport	*aeropuerto*	single ticket	*billete de ida*
train	*tren*	return ticket	*billete de ida y vuelta*
bus	*autobús*		
station	*estación de autobúses*	seat	*asiento*
		car	*coche*
boat	*barca*	petrol	*gasolina*
port	*puerto*	where is...?	*¿dónde está....?*

yes	*sí*	excuse me	*perdóneme*
no	*no*	you're welcome	*de nada*
please	*por favor*	do you speak English?	*¿hablá ingles?*
thank you	*gracias*		
welcome	*bienvenido*	how much?	*¿cuánto?*
hello	*hola*	open	*abierto*
goodbye	*adiós*	closed	*cerrado*
good morning	*buenos días*	today	*hoy*
good afternoon	*buenas tardes*	tomorrow	*mañana*
goodnight	*buenas noches*	help!	*ayuda!*

Acknowledgements

The Automobile Association wishes to thank the following photographers, libraries, associations and individuals for their assistance in the preparation of this book. **ANDALUCIA SLIDE LIBRARY** (Michelle Chaplow) 21b, 38, 39, 40b, 51, 52, 53, 73b, 77, 81a, 82a, 83a, 85, 89a, 117b; **NATURE PHOTOGRAPHERS LTD** 12a (T Wharton), 12c (S C Bisserot); **MUSEO SALZILLO** 14b;**PICTURES COLOUR LIBRARY** 48; **WORLD PICTURES LTD** 64b; www.euro.ecb.int 119 (euro notes).

The remaining photographs are held in the Association's own photo library (**AA PHOTO LIBRARY**) and were taken by Michelle Chaplow with the exception of the following:
Peter Baker 15a, 16a, 17a, 18a, 19a, 20a, 22a, 23a, 24a, 25a, 26a; Pete Bennett F/cover bottom; Jerry Edmanson F/cover (e) sunflower, B/cover Castle Almansa, 5a, 6a, 6b, 7a, 7c, 8a, 8c, 10a, 10b, 11, 12b, 14a, 20b, 27a, 28, 29, 30, 33, 35a, 40a, 40c, 49a, 50a, 54, 82b, 83b; Alex Kouprianoff F/cover (a) oranges; Eric Meacher 40d, 41b; Ken Paterson 18c, 27b; J A Tims 7b, 83c, 91a, 92, 93, 94, 95, 96, 97, 98, 99, 100, 101, 102, 103, 104, 105, 106, 107, 108, 109, 110, 111, 112, 113, 114, 115, 116; Wyn Voysey 91b; Phil Wood F/cover (d) palm tree
The photographer, Michelle Chaplow, would also like to thank the Valencian Tourist Board for all their help.

Copy editor: Hilary Hughes   **Page layout:** Design 23
Revision management: Outcrop Publishing Services, Cumbria

Dear Essential Traveller

Your comments, opinions and recommendations are very important to us. So please help us to improve our travel guides by taking a few minutes to complete this simple questionnaire.

You do not need a stamp (unless posted outside the UK). If you do not want to cut this page from your guide, then photocopy it or write your answers on a plain sheet of paper.

Send to: **The Editor, AA World Travel Guides, FREEPOST SCE 4598, Basingstoke RG21 4GY.**

Your recommendations…

We always encourage readers' recommendations for restaurants, nightlife or shopping – if your recommendation is used in the next edition of the guide, we will send you a ***FREE*** AA *Essential* **Guide** of your choice. Please state below the establishment name, location and your reasons for recommending it.

_____

_____

_____

_____

Please send me **AA *Essential*** _____

(*see list of titles inside the front cover*)

About this guide…

Which title did you buy?

AA *Essential* _____

Where did you buy it? _____

When? m m / y y

Why did you choose an AA *Essential* Guide? _____

_____

_____

_____

_____

Did this guide meet your expectations?

Exceeded ☐   Met all ☐   Met most ☐   Fell below ☐

Please give your reasons _____

_____

_____

_____

continued on next page…

Were there any aspects of this guide that you particularly liked? _____
_____
_____
_____

Is there anything we could have done better? _____
_____
_____
_____
_____

About you...

Name (*Mr/Mrs/Ms*) _____
   Address _____
_____
_____ Postcode _____
   Daytime tel nos _____

Which age group are you in?
   Under 25 ☐ 25–34 ☐ 35–44 ☐ 45–54 ☐ 55–64 ☐ 65+ ☐

How many trips do you make a year?
   Less than one ☐ One ☐ Two ☐ Three or more ☐

Are you an AA member? Yes ☐ No ☐

About your trip...

When did you book? m m / y y   When did you travel? m m / y y
How long did you stay? _____
Was it for business or leisure? _____
Did you buy any other travel guides for your trip?
   If yes, which ones? _____
_____

Thank you for taking the time to complete this questionnaire. Please send
   it to us as soon as possible, and remember, you do not need a stamp
   (*unless posted outside the UK*).

Happy Holidays!